MINDFULNESS OCD WORKBOOK

MINDFULNESS OCD

workbook

Effective Mindfulness Strategies to
Help You Manage Intrusive Thoughts

Robin Taylor Kirk, LMFT
Sarah Fader

ROCKRIDGE
PRESS

For general information on our other products and services or to obtain technical support, please contact our Customer Care Department within the United States at (866) 744-2665, or outside the United States at (510) 253-0500.

Rockridge Press publishes its books in a variety of electronic and print formats. Some content that appears in print may not be available in electronic books, and vice versa.

Interior and Cover Designer: Heather Krakora
Art Producer: Hannah Dickerson
Editor: Crystal Nero
Production Editor: Ruth Sakata Corley

Decorative art courtesy of Shutterstock, iStock
Author photo of Robin Taylor Kirk courtesy of Patricia Rose Photography
Author photo of Sarah Fader courtesy of Aaron J. Smith

ISBN: Print 978-1-64739-238-3 | eBook 978-1-64739-380-9

R0

To my mom who is and always will be my hero.

—Robin Taylor Kirk, LMFT

This book is dedicated to my children, Ari and Samara, who inspire me to keep going every day.

—Sarah Fader

This book is also dedicated to people living with OCD. You are more than your thoughts. We hope that by learning the exercises on these pages and using mindfulness, you will find a sense of grounding and confidence.

CONTENTS

• • •

INTRODUCTION

. . . .

You may be among the many people with Obsessive-Compulsive Disorder (OCD) who feel trapped by their thoughts and unable to imagine a way to find peace. It can feel as if your mind is torturing you. People with the best of intentions might say, "Just think of something else" or "Think logically; there's nothing to worry about." Oh, if you could only think of something else. This experience can be difficult to describe to someone without OCD or who has not experienced intense anxiety. It can feel devastatingly lonely. We decided to write this book because we have experienced anxiety in our own ways and have benefited greatly from mindfulness.

I'm Sarah Fader. I'm a mother of two, ages 9 and 11. I'm the author of 14 books and the CEO of the mental health nonprofit organization Stigma Fighters. I have been a mental health advocate for more than a decade. I live with OCD. As someone who has lived with Obsessive-Compulsive Disorder, I understand the challenges of navigating the condition. I have been through Cognitive Behavioral Therapy (CBT) and have been practicing mindfulness meditation for 20 years. I was introduced to Jon Kabat-Zinn (who helped bring mindfulness to the Western world) during my senior year of high school, when I was coping with intrusive thoughts from OCD and anxiety. I learned to use mindfulness and mindfulness meditation to help me navigate intrusive thoughts. It wasn't easy at first, but I have found that I am less distressed now when I experience symptoms of OCD because I have tools to manage them. Mindfulness-based practices have helped me tremendously. I was thrilled when asked to coauthor this book with OCD specialist Robin Kirk, LMFT. Though I know a lot about the condition, I have learned so much from Robin. I hope that using this workbook provides you with the tools you need to cope with OCD.

I'm Robin Taylor Kirk, LMFT, and I have been in the mental health field for 25 years. Anxiety, particularly social anxiety, is something with which I am very familiar. I can remember things like walking along the outside of open spaces and refusing to cut across because I didn't want people to notice me, and delaying graduate school after I heard that it was necessary to interview in front of a panel as part of the application process. I also began a mindfulness meditation practice about 25 years ago. It has transformed my life both personally and professionally in how I practice psychotherapy. I absolutely love what I do, which is helping people experience whatever is present in the moment without struggling and be able to get back into their lives, do things they've always wanted to do, or be more engaged and attentive with things they are already doing. It's exciting and rewarding to help people with OCD live lives that previously seemed unattainable and even unimaginable. My interest in meditation continues, and I'm a student in the two-year Mindfulness Meditation Teacher Certification Program of the Greater Good Science Center at UC Berkeley. I consider it a privilege to learn from teachers Jack Kornfield, PhD, and Tara Brach, PhD. I also volunteer with the Buddhist Pathways Prison Project teaching meditation to inmates. I have very much enjoyed working with Sarah and know that our intention throughout the writing of this workbook has been to provide exercises that will help alleviate suffering.

The Mindfulness/ OCD Connection

WHAT IS OCD? ···

Obsessive-Compulsive Disorder (OCD) is a mental health disorder in which a person experiences obsessions and compulsions that arise from the fear of acting on intrusive thoughts—not the desire to act out these thoughts. The disorder can be mild, it can interfere with living a desired life, or it can be debilitating. An obsession can be an intrusive, unwanted, or repetitive thought, disturbing visual image, or an urge that the person has trouble resisting. Compulsions are behaviors or mental acts performed to try to end the anxiety caused by an obsession. In the moment, the individual believes they will feel relief after engaging in the compulsion. One of the difficulties that people with OCD encounter is that compulsions *do* provide relief, even if it is only momentary relief. And, much of the time, that relief can feel worth it when you don't know what else to do. Our intention is to help you know what to do, particularly with respect to your thoughts.

Many of us have had intrusive and unwanted thoughts, but that doesn't mean we have OCD. Obsessive-Compulsive Disorder is a clinical diagnosis based on a pattern of behaviors. For someone to be diagnosed with OCD, they must experience obsessions and compulsions to the extent that they take up more than an hour a day or cause clinically significant impairment in areas of functioning. Here are examples of some of those obsessive thoughts and compulsions.

> **"What if" thoughts:** These are thoughts in which the individual with OCD worries about possible disastrous outcomes of a situation. An example is "What if someone put poison in my bottle of water, I drink it, and then get sick or die?"

> **Avoidance compulsion:** An avoidance compulsion is one where the individual with OCD avoids situations where they perceive danger. For example, the aforementioned individual would avoid drinking the water by throwing it out. In another situation, someone might stop themselves from stepping on a sidewalk crack because they're afraid something terrible will happen if they do step on it.

> **Thought compulsion:** These thoughts are intended to reduce a person's anxiety. Thought compulsions may include planning in advance or mentally reviewing a situation. When we speak of thoughts, we are referring to mental events that include images. A review of a situation can include bringing images to mind, such as picturing the garage door and imagining yourself looking at its bottom and sides to be sure it closed all the way so that no one can get into the house. The purpose of this is to eliminate uncertainty.

Approach compulsion: This is a behavior that involves doing something to avoid the anxiety caused by the obsession. For example, someone with contamination OCD might wash their hands repeatedly and for long periods of time until they become cracked or perhaps even bleed, in the hope of being absolutely sure that all germs have been washed away. An individual with a fear of intruders may repeatedly check to be sure the doors and windows are locked, but then feel compelled to get out of bed to check just one more time.

These are a small sampling of the common thoughts and behaviors of an individual with OCD. We'll explore ways to cope with these ideas and actions throughout this workbook.

MINDFULNESS 101

Mindfulness is the practice of experiencing the present moment without trying to push unpleasant thoughts, feelings, or sensations away or hold on to pleasant things. One of the aspects of mindfulness is developing the ability to direct one's focus of attention. Imagine the relief of being able to turn your attention away from spinning thought compulsions and back to the present. This isn't a forcing away, but rather a gentle guiding to something else, something happening in the present moment—which is the only moment we have. Practicing mindfulness can give you that freedom. A big part of mindfulness is about focusing on "right now" and letting go of control. There is so much in life that we don't have control over, and that's where mindfulness can help. You can't fix the past or know what's going to happen in the future. Sitting with your thoughts can help you learn to focus and gain clarity on how you think and feel.

THE KEY PILLARS OF MINDFULNESS

The roots of mindfulness can be found in Hinduism and Buddhism, both of which include meditation in their practices. People have been meditating for thousands of years. Hinduism incorporates yoga and Vedic meditation. In Buddhism, meditation is one aspect of the Eightfold Path to eliminate suffering.

Beginner's Mind

Beginner's mind is also known as Shoshin, a word from Zen Buddhism. It involves viewing the world with a fresh perspective, free from preconceptions. A person adopting this mentality is open to new possibilities and is ready to learn.

Non-judgment

When you're nonjudgmental, you're being an impartial observer of your own experiences. You're able to observe the comings and goings of your thoughts and physical sensations without trying to change them. For someone with OCD, there is pain in the initial feeling of anxiety that arises in response to an obsessive thought. Suffering occurs when you attempt to control that experience of anxiety. When you practice non-judgment, you're looking at your experiences from a bird's-eye view and you're not judging what you're thinking or feeling in any way.

Acceptance

Acceptance is viewing things as they are in that moment. It doesn't mean being resigned to an unwanted fate; it simply means accepting that what is happening at this moment is real. Acceptance doesn't lead to inaction; on the contrary, it can give you the clarity to take actions that need to be taken.

Patience

It's important to remember that some things unfold over time. It can be difficult for someone with OCD to be patient and allow themselves to experiment with different approaches because compulsions provide temporary relief from distress that can be debilitating. We often strive for instant gratification and want things to happen right away, but that's not always realistic. Remember that learning a new way of relating to anxiety takes time and practice.

Trust

It's important to pay attention to and trust your experience. You may think that engaging in compulsions in just the right way will allow you to finally relax. If you trust in your experience, you'll likely notice that you don't actually relax, because another obsession arises. Trust in the process of mindfulness. As you progress through this workbook, pay attention to your experience and see if the anxiety dissipates on its own once you give up the struggle to change it.

Non-striving

Non-striving involves relinquishing the need to control internal experiences. In a situation in which you begin to feel anxious, there's an immediate feeling of urgency to calm down. Instead of frantically attempting to get rid of the anxiety, non-striving can help you meet this feeling with a technique called "urge surfing," which allows you to sit with the emotion and ride it out. Just as you can't control the ocean, you can't control your thoughts—but you can ride with the waves to bring balance back to your body.

Letting Go

This mindfulness principle encourages you to let things be without grasping for more of what you like or pushing away things that are unpleasant. Imagine that you're on vacation and watching the sunset from the beach. Initially, everything seems fine, but as the sun sinks toward the horizon you start to wish it would never end and dread going back to work. These thoughts ruin the joy of a beautiful sunset. Instead, you could soak in each moment and move on to the next experience as it unfolds.

MANAGING INTRUSIVE THOUGHTS

There are several different ways to approach the treatment of OCD, and although we'll be focused on mindfulness-based techniques, it's useful to be familiar with other forms of help.

Cognitive Behavioral Therapy (CBT)

CBT focuses on changing the content of a person's thoughts, which then results in a modification of their behavior. People learn to identify cognitive distortions and to reframe their thoughts in less distorted ways. For example, imagine someone is afraid to ride in an elevator. They're convinced that if they ride in one, they'll get trapped and die. The thought includes the cognitive distortion of catastrophizing (believing something terrible is going to happen when there is no evidence to that effect). A CBT therapist would have the person write down in a thought record the actual likelihood of dying in an elevator, identify the cognitive distortion present in their thinking, and learn to replace the thought with a more functional and accurate one.

Exposure and Response Prevention (ERP)

There are two types of exposure therapy. One focuses on becoming desensitized to the anxiety trigger. The other uses mindfulness to change one's response to anxiety. We will be delving into this in more depth later in the workbook. Both types of exposure may be done in a few different contexts, including:

In vivo exposure: In vivo exposure is exposure to a trigger experienced in real life. For example, a mom who experiences contamination OCD (in her case, germs) and who wants to be able to play outside with her children or take them to the playground might walk barefoot on grass.

Imaginal exposure: In imaginal exposure, the person envisions the anxiety-producing situation. In the case of the mother with contamination OCD, she might envision her child touching playground equipment and the germs that might be on it, then the germs being transferred to the seat of the car and to anyone else who sits in that seat.

Interoceptive exposure: In interoceptive exposure, the person induces a physical sensation that is one of their symptoms of anxiety or panic. For example, perhaps the mom in the playground tends to get even more anxious when she feels her pulse quicken. As soon as that happens, she begins to think desperate thoughts about how her heart will start racing, a panic attack will come on, and not only will she be embarrassed in front of the other moms, but she won't be able to drive her daughter home. In interoceptive exposure, this mom might do jumping jacks until her heart rate is up to a level that typically brings up fear that the anxiety is bad and will get worse. She would then sit down and experience her heart rate returning to normal on its own.

Virtual reality exposure: Virtual reality exposure can help clients experience the sensations of something they're afraid of without that thing being physically present. It can also be a way to lead up to in vivo exposure. For example, imagine a person who becomes anxious in crowded places, because of the obsessive thought that someone might steal their wallet or that they won't be able to get out in an emergency. A therapist could help them work through those fears by using virtual reality equipment that simulates the sights and sounds of a crowd.

Acceptance and Commitment Therapy (ACT)

The ACT model for treatment is focused on helping people get unstuck from the ways that limit living a personally meaningful and fulfilling life. ACT can be distilled into the saying "**A**ccept your reactions and be present, **C**hoose a valued direction, and **T**ake action." As in mindfulness (which is a component of ACT), emphasis is placed on giving up trying to control your internal experience. The core elements of ACT are:

1. **Self as context:** This is seeing yourself in changing contexts. You're a changing person who is responding to context. In Western culture, views such as seeing one-self as a smart person are usually viewed as good self-esteem. But the need to hold on to that view can actually be limiting. Suppose you want to take a class in something completely unfamiliar. You might not sign up for fear of not catching on as quickly as the other students, thereby challenging your view of yourself as a smart person. There's a learning curve for information. Even things that we think of as boosting our self-esteem can be limiting.

2. **Mindfulness:** This is experiencing the present moment, not trying to change or control what's happening, and paying attention in a particular way. Attention needs to be flexible. If you play video games, you might be thinking, "Hey, I'm good at this. I'm completely dialed in when I'm playing." Although that might very well be true, if you're so dialed in that you don't notice the smell of smoke in your house, you're not paying attention in a flexible way.

3. **Defusion:** This is being able to see thoughts as what they are—just thoughts. They are not necessarily helpful, important, or meaningful. You learn to make a conscious choice as to which thoughts to follow up on, rather than blindly following up on every idea that comes to mind. This allows you to make more conscious decisions that will help you lead the life you want.

4. **Values:** These are characteristics that you want to have as an individual and they relate to how you want to show up in the world. Values are helpful not only in making decisions about what to do, but also in supporting you in relating to your anxiety in a different way.

5. **Creative hopelessness:** This is the willingness to try something different. The hopelessness isn't that *you* are hopeless, but rather that the things you have been trying have not been working. This workbook will present some creative and radically different alternatives.

As you go through this workbook, you will be using some components of ACT as you learn how to detach from thoughts in a nonjudgmental way.

Mindfulness-Based Interventions

Mindfulness returns you to the present, makes thoughts less "sticky," and makes the physical sensations of anxiety less scary. Anxiety is all about the future, so finding a way to come back to the present can be a huge relief. Many of the exercises in this workbook are designed to help you learn how to do that.

HOW TO USE THIS WORKBOOK ·····················

In this book, you will learn foundational mindfulness skills to help you live life in the moment. You will practice exercises that teach you how to let go, relinquish control of internal experiences, and be in the present moment. By participating in the exercises, you will develop the power to step away from your thoughts and look at them objectively, choosing which are deserving of your time and attention.

The book is organized by the core mindfulness principles discussed previously: beginner's mind, non-judgment, acceptance, patience, trust, non-striving, and letting go. Each of these tenets supports mindfulness in a fundamental way and can dramatically change the life of a person who has OCD. Everyone (not just people with OCD) has unpleasant or intrusive thoughts, but just because you have a thought doesn't mean you have to act on it. Mindfulness teaches us to hear our thoughts without being compelled to act on them. Let's say you're walking down the street and you have an obsessive thought. You don't have to change the thought or make it go away. You can learn to keep walking and allow the thought to be there, letting it dissipate on its own.

This workbook contains a variety of exercises designed to help you learn about and strengthen your ability to use mindfulness to alleviate thought compulsions. The exercises include both informal mindfulness practices and more formal meditation practices. No experience is required! You'll be guided all the way. You'll also find areas for personal reflection about the exercises and about the material in the workbook. Freedom from thought compulsions is absolutely possible, and we encourage you to participate fully in each of the activities to discover this for yourself. Consider doing the exercises as an experiment in finding what works best for you.

You don't have to follow the workbook chronologically. If it helps, you can work through different chapters at a time. It's okay to focus on the areas of mindfulness that you feel will be the most beneficial to whatever you're dealing with at the moment.

It's essential to note that this workbook is a complementary tool to other work you are doing to respond differently to intrusive thoughts. It is in no way meant to replace therapy or any mental health treatment that you're currently engaged in to treat your OCD; instead, use the book as a supplement to enhance the great work you're already doing. It can be beneficial to show this workbook to your therapist and discuss what you have found to be helpful. If you are not in therapy, we encourage you to find a therapist who specializes in OCD. There are several places to search for experienced therapists in your area, including IOCDF.org, ADAA.org, and PsychologyToday.com. If you are unable to leave your home, or if there are no specialized therapists in your area, try finding a therapist who offers teletherapy; it is becoming a more and more common treatment option.

BEFORE YOU BEGIN

The exercises in the workbook are activities that you can incorporate into your daily life. They're not meant to take away from what you're already doing to ease your symptoms of OCD, but rather to support you. You can do each exercise in 10 to 20 minutes a day. Although it's most effective if you practice these exercises on a daily basis, don't feel like you have to do them every day. You can set aside particular days to practice if that's easier for you. Just remember that you'll get out of it what you put into it. If you keep practicing the exercises, you'll get better and better at them and you'll notice results more quickly.

We understand that doing these exercises might be a difficult process. Human beings are excellent problem solvers. We don't have claws and we can't run fast; our superpower is problem solving. Our ancestors didn't enjoy getting rained on, so they learned how to build shelters to protect themselves. Now, if we're cold, we can turn up the heat in the house. However, thinking that we can manage our internal environment in the same way we are often able to manage the external environment can lead to trouble. Struggling against internal thoughts and sensations usually intensifies and prolongs them—just the opposite of what we hope for. It can be counterintuitive to someone with OCD or another anxiety disorder, but loosening the grip allows the anxiety to dissipate naturally.

This workbook and the practices within it can transform your relationship with your thoughts. It can be helpful when doing challenging exercises to remember why doing them is important to you. In the space provided, write down three things you'd like to do after completing the workbook that you avoid doing now or don't enjoy doing now because of being preoccupied with thought compulsions.

1. _____

_____

_____

_____

2. _____

_____

_____

_____

_____

_____

_____

_____

3. _____

_____

_____

_____

_____

_____

_____

_____

This workbook is all about you gaining freedom to live a life that's full and meaningful to you, which includes doing the things you just listed. Stick with it, and get ready to reap the benefits.

THE MINDFUL ATTENTION AWARENESS SCALE (MAAS) ADAPTED FOR OCD ················

The Mindfulness Attention Awareness Scale (MAAS) will give you an indication of your current degree of mindfulness. A higher score indicates a higher degree of mindfulness. There isn't a threshold above which your score is supposed to be, but this adapted scale will help give you a snapshot of where you are now. To complete the scale, please give your answers in terms of how you have felt over the past week.

Rate the following statements on a scale from 1 to 6.
1: almost always 2: very frequently 3: somewhat frequently
4: somewhat infrequently 5: very infrequently 6: almost never

_____ 1. I might feel an uncomfortable emotion and not be conscious of it until later.

_____ 2. I'm distracted and forget where I put things like my keys or my bag.

_____ 3. I'm often lost in the past or the future.

_____ 4. When walking, I'm usually unaware of my surroundings.

_____ 5. I have a vague sense of discomfort in my body, but it's difficult to identify the sensations.

_____ 6. I often find it difficult to pay attention in conversations.

_____ 7. I'm on autopilot most of the time.

_____ 8. When I'm doing something, I'm thinking of the next thing I have to accomplish.

_____ 9. It's difficult to focus on what I'm doing in the moment because I want to get to the end.

_____ 10. I do compulsive behaviors automatically.

_____ 11. I only listen with one ear because I'm preoccupied with my thoughts.

_____ 12. I walk into a room and then forget why I'm there.

_____ 13. I will look down and see an empty plate, hardly having been aware of eating or of the taste of the food.

_____ 14. I feel the need to push away disturbing thoughts so that I can pay attention.

_____ 15. I get lost in thought compulsions and time goes by without my realizing it.

Total score of the 15 items: _____

We'll revisit this scale at the end of the workbook so you can see how your score has changed. This isn't a contest and there isn't any minimum amount of improvement you should be aiming for. This is simply a tool you can use to help you appreciate change over time.

CHAPTER 2

Beginner's Mind

THE CHALLENGE ·

Although it may seem counterintuitive, mindfulness can have a beneficial effect for those with OCD. It can be very unpleasant, to say the least, to experience repetitive, intrusive, and disturbing thoughts and images in your mind. Using mindfulness can alleviate the resulting distress. People with OCD understandably feel an urgency to take action in order to rid themselves of the anxiety. When you practice mindfulness, you learn to be with your thoughts and urges and not engage in compulsions. We're going to work on some exercises that will help you practice being with your thoughts and observing them without passing judgment on them. It might seem difficult, but there are ways that you can free yourself from the cycle of shame connected to intrusive thoughts.

Common Obsessive Thoughts

Throughout this workbook, we'll look at a variety of obsessive thoughts. You may recognize some or all of them. Intrusive thoughts often reflect some common subject matter themes. These "What if?" thoughts might take one or more of the following forms:

Contamination: These "What if" thoughts include coming in contact with either germs or environmental contaminants, such as household cleaners or possible radiation from cell phones.

> What if my child plays near a power line and contracts cancer?

> I'm at a restaurant and I can't stop thinking about whether the food is safe to eat. What if I get sick because the waiter didn't wash his hands?

> I used a public restroom, and I'm convinced that I contracted an STD by sitting on the toilet seat even though I used four seat covers. What if I was careless and I now have an STD?

Harm (to self or others): These "What if" thoughts include causing harm either intentionally or negligently to oneself or others.

> I didn't push my chair all the way in at the restaurant. What if someone trips over it and gets hurt because of me?

What if I lose control and cut myself?

I didn't put enough carrots in my husband's salad. What if his eyesight goes bad and it's my fault?

What if I blurt out a racial slur while in the grocery store?

Sexuality: These "What if" thoughts relate to fears about being straight if gay and vice versa, being attracted to a member of one's own family, or being a pedophile. It is important to understand, especially when discussing socially taboo subject matter, that OCD is a *fear* of doing something, not a desire to do something.

What if I'm attracted to my father/mother/sister/brother?

I'm a man and I just thought "That's a good-looking guy." Does that mean I'm gay?

A woman was wearing a very low-cut top and I looked at her breasts. What if that means I'm not really a gay man and shouldn't be with my partner?

What if I'm sexually attracted to children?

Relationships: These obsessions involve fears that one or the other partner is not or does not want to be faithful and/or that the relationship isn't the "right" one.

My partner didn't hug me back as hard as I hugged her. What if she doesn't love me or want to be with me?

What if being irritated with my partner means I don't love him?

I made eye contact with my coworker. What if that means I want to be with him and not my husband?

I called my wife and it went to voice mail. She didn't call back for 20 minutes. What if she's with some guy and cheating on me?

Immorality/Sin/Sacrilege: These "What if" thoughts include fears about being disrespectful to God, committing a sin, saying something that isn't 100 percent accurate or leaves something out, behaving at all rudely, not praying correctly, or not helping those in need.

What if my mind wandered during church?

What if I blurt out something blasphemous?

What if I disrespect Jesus by not looking at his picture while praying?

I didn't go back and tell the store clerk she gave me too much change. What if God exacts retribution against someone I love?

Claudia's Story

It can be comforting to know that most people have intrusive, unwanted thoughts. For example, Robin was in the bathroom getting ready one morning. She glanced at a pair of scissors, and the thought "What if I pick those up and stab myself in the eye?" went through her mind. Because she doesn't have OCD, she recognized that the thought didn't have any real meaning; it was just weird and she could shake her head and continue getting ready.

If Robin had OCD, the thought would seem to be meaningful. In other words, if she had this thought it must mean something and therefore she would need to take action, specifically action to make sure she didn't lose control and stab herself in the eye (remember that obsessions are *fears* of doing something, not *desires* to do something). She might ask her partner to lock up all the scissors. But wait, what about knives? She might be cooking and lose control. So they lock up all the knives. Susie invites Robin over, but she can't go because Susie has scissors and knives in her home. Life becomes smaller and smaller as avoidance grows.

Claudia, a new mother, is putting her baby to sleep but he won't stop crying. She has an intrusive thought that she might hit him. She doesn't actually want to harm her child, but the thought is very upsetting. She's so plagued by the guilt and shame of the thought that she doesn't know what to do. She doesn't think she can tell anyone; she's certain that they'd take her baby away. The only thing she can think to do is stay away from her baby or always have someone else in the house. For a while, her mother comes over during the day, but she soon loses patience with the arrangement.

How can this mother help herself?

Instead of punishing herself for the intrusive thought, she can recognize that the thought is a product of OCD. She can sit with the thought instead of trying to change it. Eventually it will go away and she can continue caring for her child as she normally would.

MEDITATION ON SOUND

The idea of meditation can be daunting. Simply put, meditation is a way of training your mind to attend to your experience in the present moment, to experience the physical sensations of anxiety in a way that is less scary, and to get some space from thoughts that make your mind spin. You've probably noticed that anxiety is all about the future. With practice, disengaging from anxious thoughts and coming back to the present becomes easier and easier. Although meditation is most valuable if practiced daily, it is still beneficial when practiced less frequently; however, change will likely occur more slowly. Be patient with yourself when learning this new skill.

Mindfulness meditation often involves paying attention to physical sensations, such as the breath. This can be challenging for people with OCD because the breath can be subtle and turning toward inner experience is often not one's first choice. We'll start with a meditation on sound to begin developing the skill of moment-to-moment awareness. As with all the guided meditations in this book, you may either read it through several times and then do the meditation or record it on your phone and play it back while doing the meditation.

Find a place where you will be undisturbed. Begin by setting a timer for 10 minutes. You may use any timer, but the Insight Timer app is a wonderful tool because it allows you to settle in before the timer starts and ends the session with a bell, so there's no jarring alarm that needs to be turned off immediately. If you are in a place with background noise, great. If not, you might want to play instrumental music in the background.

Sit with your back straight but not rigid and your chin parallel with the ground, as though there's a string pulling you gently up from the top of your head. This will help with both alertness and attention. You may close your eyes, or if that's not comfortable, you may keep your eyes open and maintain a soft gaze at the floor a couple of feet in front of you. Notice the points of contact of your body with the couch or sofa, feeling how you are supported by it. In your own time, turn your attention to the sounds in your environment. There's no need to struggle to hear or identify a particular sound; just imagine opening your ears and allowing the sounds in, experiencing the tone, volume, and movement of each one, being with them as they are and as they change moment to moment. Each time your mind wanders, gently guide your attention back to the experience of the sounds. Initially, you may need to do this frequently, and at first it might feel as if you're doing it every second or two. With time and practice, this will change. If one stops stirring a glass of water with dirt in it, the dirt will settle at the bottom and you'll have clear water. The same is true of the mind: With time and practice, the mind settles.

EXERCISE 1: *YOU* AREN'T THE PROBLEM

Anxiety, particularly intense anxiety, is painful. People naturally try to stay away from things that cause pain because the avoidance of pain helps our survival in the physical world. If something bites you and your arm swells up and turns red, pain is the signal that something needs to be done, such as going to see a medical professional. We tend to react the same way to the pain in our internal world (thoughts, emotions, sensations, and urges). Let's take a look at what you've tried previously in order to get rid of your anxiety. In the space provided, list the things you've done in the past. These might include "positive" things, such as yoga and progressive muscle relaxation, as well as "negative" things, such as trying to talk yourself out of it or doing excessive research on a topic. Next to each attempt at control, put a check under "Short Term" if it helped in the short term (i.e., a few minutes to a few days) or under "Long Term" if it was effective at eliminating anxiety in the long term.

ATTEMPT AT CONTROL	SHORT TERM	LONG TERM

If your experience is like that of most people, your attempts at control have been effective in the short term but don't provide long-term relief. It can be so frustrating to know that you're an intelligent person, you've tried everything you can think of to make this anxiety go away, but nothing works in the way you want it to. You might think that you're the problem. But consider this: Perhaps *you* aren't the problem, but the methods you've been trying are the problem. It's worth taking a moment to let that sink in. Reading the list of things you've tried might feel discouraging, but it's actually hopeful because it means there's another possibility. Why not try doing something radically different and find out?

What thoughts or emotions came up for you during this exercise?

_____

_____

_____

_____

_____

_____

_____

_____

_____

_____

_____

_____

_____

_____

_____

_____

_____

_____

_____

_____

_____

EXERCISE 2: NAME YOUR OCD

Bringing a kind and present attitude to your OCD can seem like a wild idea. Often, people are told to "fight their OCD bully" or something similar. Maybe that expression is helpful for you, or maybe it seems as if it puts you at war with yourself. OCD is not something outside you; it's one of the ways your brain functions at this time. Remember when we mentioned we'd suggest some very different approaches? This is one of them: What if you brought some kind and gentle attention to your anxiety? What if you gave your OCD a sweet name? We'll use "Barney" in this example. What if you thought of Barney as a scared young child who is terrified of the things your OCD focuses on? Barney isn't out to get you, he is just scared. Yelling at him or fighting with him is not going to make him feel one bit less anxious. If a young child is afraid, isn't it most helpful to hold him and let him know you're there with him, that he doesn't have to go through it alone? The next time you feel anxious, experiment with talking to your anxiety kindly. Let that frightened part of yourself know that you understand it's scared and that you'll be there for it as you continue.

What's your name for your OCD and how might you be kind to it?

EXERCISE 3: POPCORN POPPER

We will suggest in this workbook several ways to work with obsessions and thought compulsions. The optimal way to approach these is to try each suggestion at least a few times to determine if it's one that resonates with and is helpful for you.

Sometimes the thoughts come fast and furiously. It can be hard just to identify the thoughts, much less work with them, when the anxiety is high. When this happens, try this exercise, which can be helpful in these circumstances. Begin by setting a timer for 5 minutes. Get into a comfortable position and close your eyes. Imagine that your head is an air-pop popcorn machine with the lid off. The popper is turned on and the kernels are heating up. They start popping and flying all over the place. Now imagine that the kernels represent your thoughts. You don't need to place each thought in a kernel; they automatically attach and fly. The good news is that they're popped by hot air and so can land anywhere without hurting anything. They can land on furniture, on the floor, and even on you and not hurt a thing. They can just be. When the timer sounds, take a few breaths to reorient yourself.

Observing your thoughts in this kind of nonjudgmental way can help loosen their grip and can remove some of the urgency and seriousness that come with them. As with the other experiential exercises in this workbook, set aside time on a regular basis to practice for 5 minutes. We always have thoughts with which to practice; they don't have to be anxiety-related. Honing your skill with this on a regular basis makes it much easier to use when your thoughts are racing.

Encouraging Words

There will be challenges during the process of learning how to use mindfulness to work with your OCD. These are opportunities to grow and learn more about yourself and to feel empowered. You can learn to sit with your thoughts in a nonjudgmental way and work with them as opposed to fighting them. By practicing the exercises in this workbook, you'll start to notice a difference in the way you view your thoughts and will find them less daunting and more neutral. You can observe your thoughts as they are, without assigning a value to them.

EXERCISE 4: THE CONVEYOR BELT

Have you ever watched the episode of *I Love Lucy* in which Lucy and Ethel are working in the candy factory? Whether you have or not, right now is a good time to put down the workbook and google *I Love Lucy candy wrapping job.* Sit back for a few minutes and let them entertain you.

Although this is a fun scene, did it perhaps remind you of what it can be like to try to control your thoughts? Let's try something a little different.

Begin by setting a timer for 5 minutes. Sit comfortably and close your eyes. Imagine that you're standing in a room that is empty except for a conveyor belt that enters the room from an opening in one wall, travels the length of the room, and exits through an opening in the opposite wall. As you stand in front of the conveyor belt, you notice that through no effort of your own, your thoughts are out of your head and going past you on the conveyor belt. They may take the form of words, shapes, or perhaps a combination of both. They may be spaced out at times and piled together at other times. There is no effort on your part. You may simply observe them moving past you and out through the opening in the wall. When the timer sounds, imagine the belt slowing down and coming to a halt and the lights dimming in the room, then bring your attention back to being seated in your chair.

EXERCISE 5: BULLET TRAIN

An option exists for working with thoughts that seem to be racing too quickly for either the popcorn popper or the conveyor belt exercise. To practice with these speeding thoughts, close your eyes and imagine that you're sitting on a hill. A bullet train flashes by at a speed of 175 miles per hour. The cars (your thoughts) go by in a blur and it's difficult to differentiate one from another, but you don't need to. You can just sit on the hill and watch the thoughts speed by. When you've practiced this for a few minutes, go ahead and open your eyes. If your thoughts are racing but you're not in a position to close your eyes right then, you might note "bullet train" to yourself and bring your attention back to the moment.

It's most helpful to practice these exercises at least a few times a week. Don't wait until you're in the middle of a high anxiety situation to try to use them to "feel better." It's best to think of these as practices that will, with time, help you get some space from your thoughts, allow them to come and go, and recognize that they're just thoughts and that you have the power to choose how to respond to them.

What did you notice when you worked with thoughts in these different ways? Did one way resonate with you more than the others? Are there any ways you might modify the exercises to make them fit your situation better?

MINDFUL MOMENT: BEGINNER'S MIND · · · · · · · · · · ·

Being open to new ideas is at the heart of Beginner's Mind. Approaching things with this mentality allows us to let go of assumptions and recognize that there is much more to know about ourselves and our experiences.

AFFIRMATION

I have the power to take a risk, even when my
mind is telling me that I don't. Change happens
when I open my mind to experiencing something new. OCD doesn't have complete power
over me. I can change, and I'm working on ways
to feel more grounded.

Non-judgment

THE CHALLENGE $\cdots\cdots\cdots\cdots\cdots\cdots\cdots\cdots\cdots\cdots\cdots\cdots\cdots\cdots\cdots$

A person with OCD will ascribe meaning and importance to a thought when in reality the thought is random. To the person struggling with OCD, it seems urgent and requires action. With mindfulness practice, you're better able to determine whether a thought is helpful or unhelpful. You can be a witness to your experience, observe your thoughts, and decide whether to act on them. For example, imagine a dad who is driving to work afraid that he'll miss an important meeting. His tires go *thud* and he wonders if he ran someone over. He checks his rearview mirror and side mirrors and doesn't see anyone. He thinks, "What if they rolled into the gutter, I didn't see them, and they need my help?" Because he can't witness his experience or sit with his thoughts, he circles the block many times looking for the person he believes he hit. He thinks, "What if they crawled into a store entrance?" He is plagued by "What if" thoughts. He carries on searching for the person for an hour, and ends up arriving late for the meeting. This isn't the first time something like this has happened, and his job might be in jeopardy.

How can mindfulness help this dad?

Instead of agonizing over the idea that he hurt someone, he could release control of his mind. If he can allow the thoughts to be there and view them as neither good nor bad, he can detach from them. It wouldn't feel as if his thoughts are dragging him around. Because he is approaching his OCD with mindfulness, he can pull over, observe the parade of thoughts nonjudgmentally, and let them dissipate on their own. He relinquishes control, stops judging himself and his thoughts, and feels a sense of relief by using mindfulness.

Common Obsessive Thoughts

Some obsessive thoughts that are common among those living with OCD involve doing something wrong that results in dire consequences. One might be afraid of accidentally committing a crime or offending someone. The thoughts can range from taboo topics to harming oneself or others. Here are some common intrusive thoughts about making an error that can plague people with OCD.

> What if I wrote an obscenity or racial slur in the email I just sent?

> What if I walk up to the checkout line and steal a candy bar?

> What if I only *think* I heard the lock click when I locked the deadbolt?

> What if I put the air conditioner in the window incorrectly and it falls on someone and kills them?

> What if I give someone the wrong amount of change and as punishment God hurts somebody I love?

Jason's Story

Jason, a father of two young girls, is convinced that he might be a pedophile. He has trouble spending time alone with his daughters because he is afraid that he might touch them inappropriately. He wonders if he touched them and didn't know it. That thought is so disgusting and terrifying to him that he cannot allow it to be in his mind for even a moment. He tries to get rid of the thought by using thought compulsions to reassure himself that his daughters have never looked at him strangely or acted frightened around him, which they would surely do had he touched them inappropriately. He repeatedly focuses on what a loyal father and husband he is to reassure himself that he would never harm his children. No matter how hard he tries, he can't seem to make his anxiety go away.

How can this dad use non-judgment to help himself?

It's common in this situation for someone to judge themselves for merely having the thought. Using mindfulness, this dad could recognize that the thought is there and then return his attention to the present. He doesn't need to change his thoughts, because, like everything, his thoughts will change. The thoughts may be disturbing, but deep down he knows they are not the truth. Instead of trying to change them, he can sit with his thoughts mindfully, observe them, and let them pass.

ICE CUBE MEDITATION ·······································

People often think that the goal of mindfulness meditation is to calm down or empty the mind. These beliefs can make meditation frustrating and lead to self-criticism: "Why can't I empty my mind when everyone else obviously can?" "I'm still anxious, I must be doing something wrong." "This will never work." Actually, the purpose of meditation is to be with whatever arises in the moment, without trying to get rid of the unpleasant, get more of the pleasant, or nod off on the neutral. Our survival as humans depended on our ability to judge whether something was dangerous (bad) or safe (good). We have carried that forward and now apply it to our internal experiences with some unfortunate results.

In this meditation, you will learn to be with something usually thought of as unpleasant (unless it's a hot summer day) while noticing the sensations and resisting the urge to change them.

Wrap a couple of pieces of ice in a paper towel and set a timer for 5 minutes. Now take a seat and maintain an upright and alert posture. Begin by holding the ice on the outside of your forearm. As best you can, feel the sensations without judging them. You might note to yourself "tingling" or "burning." See if you can feel the line of demarcation between where the ice is touching your skin and where it isn't. Leave it there for 1 minute or so. Next, move the ice to the inside of your forearm and repeat the process, mindfully noting the sensations for 1 minute or so. If you feel the urge to move the ice early, notice the urge and how it feels in your body, but see if you can keep the ice where it is. Now move the ice to the inside of your elbow where the sensations may be more intense, and experience the sensations, without trying to change them in any way, for 1 minute or so. Move the ice down to the inside of your wrist. The sensations might get quite lively here; everyone is different in terms of where they feel them most intensely. Again, take 1 minute and experience what is present. Finally, move the ice to your palm and be with what is there. The intention of this meditation is to experience sensations as they are and as they change moment to moment.

Take a moment to write down anything you noticed during the mindfulness meditation, including anything that surprised you about it.

_____

_____

_____

_____

_____

_____

_____

_____

_____

_____

_____

_____

_____

_____

_____

Many of us don't associate physical sensations with emotions, but they are always a part of emotion, even if we don't recognize it. The sensations accompanying OCD can be quite unpleasant, to say the least. It is extremely helpful to begin practicing observing what's happening in your body without trying to change it. This makes anxiety much less frightening and helps relieve the urgency to get rid of it. The next four exercises focus on how emotions affect the body.

EXERCISE 1: EMOTIONS IN THE BODY: SADNESS

Sit in an upright and alert posture and close your eyes. Bring to mind a time in the recent past when you felt sadness. Don't choose an extremely sad event, because it's easier to notice things when the emotion is less intense. See the event playing out in your mind as if you were plunked down into a movie of it—who was there, what the room or space was like, what sounds and voices you heard—making the event as real as possible. As you keep the scene in mind, set your attention on your body. What physical sensations do you notice? (As in the Ice Cube Meditation [see page 35], this noticing should be a neutral description rather than a judgment.) Where are the physical sensations located? Is there movement? Bring the curtain down on the movie, take a couple of deep breaths, and feel your seat supporting you.

Take a moment to write down the physical sensations you noticed during this exercise.

EXERCISE 2: EMOTIONS IN THE BODY: ANGER

Sit in an upright and alert posture and close your eyes. Take three breaths: in for a count of four, hold for a count of two, and out for a count of four. Now bring to mind a time in the recent past when you felt angry or irritated. Again, don't choose a situation in which you felt the most enraged you've ever felt, but rather a situation that evoked a degree of irritation or anger with which you can work. See the situation playing out in your mind's eye. When you notice feelings of anger or irritation, slow down, open yourself to the feelings, and experience them as sensations in your body. Bring the curtain down on the movie, take a couple of deep breaths, and feel your seat supporting you.

Take a moment to write down the physical sensations you noticed during this exercise.

EXERCISE 3: EMOTIONS IN THE BODY: ANXIETY

Now it's time to experiment with an emotion that you probably feel certain you know all about. After all, you've been suffering with and struggling against anxiety for a long time. Perhaps now you can experience it in a different way. Sit in an upright and alert posture, close your eyes, and feel yourself supported by your chair. Bring to mind a time when you felt mild to moderate anxiety. It can be anxiety triggered by something other than OCD. When you begin to feel the physical sensations of anxiety, turn your attention to them. Invite them in and approach them with curiosity. Where do you feel the sensations in your body? Can you describe the feelings just as sensations, without attaching judgment? Bring the curtain down on the movie, take a couple of deep breaths, and feel your seat supporting you.

Take a moment to write down the physical sensations you noticed during this exercise.

Encouraging Words

It's possible for you to experience symptoms of OCD and still enjoy your life. Those are two things that can occur at the same time. You can have intrusive thoughts and keep doing what you're doing at the moment, whether that's playing with your child, taking a walk, or doing your job at work.

How are you feeling at this moment? Take a minute to reflect and think about which emotions are moving through you. There is no wrong way to feel; all your feelings are valid.

EXERCISE 4: EMOTIONS IN THE BODY: HAPPINESS

Now, here's a slightly different take on the exercise you've been practicing. Sit in an upright and alert posture and close your eyes. Recall a time in the recent past when you felt pleased, happy, or excited about something. See the event playing out in your mind as if you were plunked down into a movie of it—who was there, what the room or space was like, what sounds and voices you heard—making the event as real as possible. When you sense happiness, drop your attention into your body and notice the physical sensations you feel related to this emotion. Bring the curtain down on the movie, take a couple of deep breaths, and feel your seat supporting you.

Take a moment to write down the physical sensations you noticed during this exercise.

EXERCISE 5: LEMON, LEMON, LEMON

Particularly with the more socially taboo obsessions (e.g., pedophilia, incest), some words in particular might be associated with disgust or anxiety. Sometimes, even writing the first letter of the word is enough to be triggering. This can, of course, occur no matter the subject of your obsessions. There can be a lot of judgment and avoidance of the word itself. Judgment about internal experiences or events and avoidance are cornerstones of OCD. Let's try something that might help neutralize charged words.

Begin by imagining a lemon. Visualize the bright yellow skin with pockmarks all over it. Imagine holding it to your nose and smelling the faint citrus scent. Now imagine yourself opening a bit of the peel and smelling that burst of lemon fragrance. Your mouth may begin watering as you read this. Now, for 1 minute, say the word "lemon" aloud as fast as you can. What did you notice at the end of the minute?

Many people find that instead of being a triggering word that makes your mouth water, after a while the word becomes one continuous sound and can actually be funny. This exercise works with other words, too. In therapy, people with a fear of being a pedophile may be encouraged to say "pedophile" over and over, and often actually end up laughing as their tongue becomes completely twisted up and some pretty funny sounds emerge. Often, after doing this exercise, the word has lost its charge.

Give it a try. Choose a word that is charged for you and repeat it as fast as you can for 1 minute. What did you notice?

MINDFUL MOMENT: NON-JUDGMENT

It's easy to fall into a pattern of guilt and shame when it comes to intrusive thoughts. You might wonder, "What's wrong with me that I had that upsetting thought?" Then the feedback loop of shame and intrusive thoughts continues. This is where nonjudgmental thinking can help. If you remove the judgment from your thoughts, the power they seemed to have vanishes. The thoughts aren't good or bad, they simply *are*. You didn't cause yourself to have any of these thoughts, they just appeared in your mind. Accept them for what they are—only thoughts—and avoid placing any kind of value on them.

People think all kinds of thoughts; however, for someone with OCD, disturbing thoughts are more significant and seem to have inherent value. It can be painful when you judge yourself for having a thought, and that judgment can lead you to engage in reassurance seeking or compulsions because you think you need to get rid of the thought. This is why looking at thoughts without judging them is crucial. Another plus is that, if you don't feel the need to make judgments about your thoughts, there's less pressure on you. You don't have to evaluate everything that goes through your mind.

AFFIRMATION

I am not my thoughts. I am a person who

has a rich life experience. I'm thinking about

one thing that I love about myself that

brings me joy.

CHAPTER 4

Acceptance

THE CHALLENGE ·····································

Acceptance can help you cope with OCD because so much of the disorder is trying to control things. When you surrender to the fact that you have limited control and accept that your thoughts are there, you can rise above the urges to act on those thoughts. Mindfulness helps you accept that the thoughts are there, that you don't have to try to change them, and that you can simply sit with them. The thoughts may feel disturbing, even frightening, but they cannot hurt you. Much of anxiety and OCD is the urge to get rid of a disturbing feeling, emotion, or bodily sensation. Rather than trying to eliminate those feelings, emotions, or sensations, accept them and keep going. It's challenging to sit with those feelings and not do anything, but doing so will help you change. Accept that the feelings are present at this moment and learn to move with them rather than try to make them go away.

Common Obsessive Thoughts

One form of intrusive thoughts involves harming oneself or others. An individual with OCD can feel disturbed by these thoughts because they're afraid they will lose control, snap, or not be able to stop the harm from happening. These thoughts can distress a person who has OCD, but using mindfulness and nonjudgmental thinking are helpful ways to cope with them. Just because you have a thought doesn't mean you have to make it go away or else run the risk of acting on it. Here are some examples of intrusive thoughts about harm.

> What if I lose my temper and punch my supervisor in the face? I'm afraid I won't be able to control myself.

> I'm afraid that I can't drive my car because no matter what I do I'll cause an accident on the road. I can't stop thinking about rear-ending someone while I'm driving.

> What if I get so mad that I hit my child and Child Protective Services takes them away?

What if I left the stove on? What if the house is burning down and all my animals are dead? I can't stop thinking about this while I'm at work and can't do my job.

I'm afraid I'm going to knock my hair dryer into the bathtub and electrocute myself.

What if I don't straighten out a rug and someone trips on it and gets hurt? How will I live with myself if that happens?

Sylvia's Story

Sylvia suffers from chronic migraines and has been prescribed medicine for her headaches. Every time she looks at the bottle of medicine, she worries that someone has tampered with it and she'll get sick or it will alter her mind in some way. She reluctantly takes her medicine, but there are times when she's too afraid to do so. She tries to reassure herself by taking it in her bag everywhere she goes so she knows that it's safe. But she worries that somehow when she wasn't looking, someone has gotten to the medicine in her purse and tampered with it. Although it's scary for her to take her medicine while she believes that someone has tampered with it, she knows that not taking it will result in her not being able to function.

How could this woman use acceptance to help herself?

She can let the thoughts be there, understand that they are intrusive thoughts, and not try to reassure herself that she is safe. Why would she not reassure herself that her medicine isn't poisoned? Because reassurance seeking is a thought compulsion and a cycle that is important to stop, which is where acceptance can help her. She doesn't have to keep telling herself that everything is fine, but rather can accept that she is anxious. By accepting that her thoughts are present, and by remembering that taking her medicine is of the utmost importance, she can do what's best for her.

WALKING MEDITATION

You are likely familiar with at least some of the feelings of being antsy, jittery, or wanting to crawl out of your skin. When it feels as though sitting to do meditation would be intolerable, a walking meditation can be a good alternative.

Walking for 10 minutes is a good place to start. Find a place where you can walk 8 to 10 feet in a straight line. Set a timer for 10 minutes. Begin by standing still, with your back straight but not rigid and your chin parallel with the ground, as though there's a string pulling you gently up from the top of your head. Your gaze should rest at the floor a couple of feet in front of you. You may either clasp your hands in front of you or have them straight at your sides. The goal is not to walk quickly or to cover ground, but to be mindfully aware of your legs and feet as you walk. As you lift and place your foot, be aware of the movement of your muscles and joints, the shifting of weight, and the pressure on the soles of your feet as you place each one on the ground. Generally, walk slowly enough to allow for the experience of the mechanics of walking. When you reach the end of your path, stop, take a couple of deep breaths, and turn around mindfully. Repeat this process until the timer sounds.

What did you notice and what are your impressions of walking meditation compared to the other meditations you've tried?

EXERCISE 1: FOOT MEDITATION ANYTIME, ANYWHERE

This activity also focuses on the feet, but in a way that can be used anytime, anywhere. When you're feeling caught up in your thought compulsions, direct your attention down to your feet. We have lots of nerve endings in our feet and there are lots of sensations going on there. We usually have on shoes and/or socks or can feel the ground or floor under our feet. Really notice and experience what's there. Feel the seams of your socks, the contact with your shoe, the differences in temperature on the points that are exposed to air and the ones that aren't. You can do this standing, sitting, or lying down. Your feet are always with you, and no one will ever know you're doing an informal mindfulness practice. By focusing your attention on your feet, experiencing and accepting the moment-to-moment changing sensations, and returning your attention to these sensations each time your thoughts and attention drift, you can come back to the present and still anxiety-driven thoughts.

EXERCISE 2: NO NEED TO PUSH AWAY YOUR THOUGHTS

The more you fight against your thoughts, the stickier they become. When you have an obsession or when you are wrapped up in thought compulsions, note "thinking" to yourself and return your attention to the present. You don't need to wrestle your attention back to the present; merely guide as much of your attention back as you can. The noting is gentle, like touching the thoughts with a feather.

It can help if your mind has something to chew on when you return your attention to the present. Using your senses to engage with the present is the most effective route available, and initially it can still be helpful to engage your verbal mind as well. Please note that this is not used as a distraction (e.g., "I don't want to think this thought so I'm going to push it away with these other thoughts."), but rather as an engagement with the present. As you take a walk, look around the room, or finish cooking dinner, experiment with internal narration. If no one is around, please feel free to do this out loud. Otherwise, you might want to narrate to yourself. Keep your mind engaged with the present by doing a play-by-play of your actions: "I'm getting a carrot out of the refrigerator." "I'm washing the carrot and feeling the water on my hands." This is especially helpful when you begin practicing mindfulness as a part of your work with OCD. As you utilize this in conjunction with regular practice of the suggestions found in this workbook, your mind will settle, you will be able to engage directly with your experience, and you will no longer need the support of narration.

What did you notice about this exercise? Did you notice any judgments?

Can you allow the judgments to be there without embracing them as truths?

EXERCISE 3: SEARS TOWER IN CHICAGO

One of the things that is important to Robin is adventure. So, when in Chicago once for a conference, she decided she wanted to go on the observation deck in Sears Tower. The building is 110 stories tall and the observation deck is on the 104th floor. Even though adventure is important, she had anxiety about falling from a high place. She felt no anxiety while walking around the floor looking out the windows, but as soon as she stood in the short line to go out onto the all-clear acrylic balcony (because how many people *really* want to step into seemingly thin air when 104 stories up?), the anxiety started. She could feel her heart starting to pound, a trickle of sweat run down her back, her hands shaking, and her knees weakening, and her thoughts started spinning: "When was this balcony last inspected?" "Do they have carnival workers assembling these things?" "Is my will up to date?" As she started getting ramped up, she remembered to practice what she preaches. She began to experience the situation mindfully. She felt the coolness on her back where the sweat had trickled down, the pounding of her heart reverberating throughout her torso, the stickiness of her clammy hands. When the thoughts raced through her mind, she would note "thinking" and return to experiencing the sensations in her body.

When you step out onto the clear balcony (yes, the floor is clear, too) you can't see the street, and so Robin had to will her leg to step out into what seemed to be thin air. Once she was there, she was so glad she hadn't run away. It's a spectacular view from a vantage point people rarely see. She even looked down, enjoying the sight of itty-bitty people on the sidewalk. Did she still have some physical sensations? Yes. Did they detract from the experience? No. And, life being what it is, a 14-year-old boy stepped out onto the balcony with her (the balcony is about as big as a couch) and started jumping up and down. That sure livened things up! But Robin was still able to feel the sensations and touch the thoughts lightly while enjoying the view.

It was only because she accepted what was present that she was able to be with her anxiety and also really enjoy the experience and view. Although Robin doesn't suffer with OCD, the anxiety was pretty strong. Can you see how you might apply this approach when coming in contact with a trigger? In the space below, please write a plan for how you might put it all together when in contact with a trigger.

_____

_____

_____

_____

_____

_____

_____

_____

_____

What do you imagine will be the most difficult thing to be with?

_____

_____

_____

_____

_____

_____

_____

_____

_____

_____

_____

Can you set the intention to stay present with it in the service of living a life that includes things that are important to you?

Encouraging Words

There is no quick solution to changing your relationship to obsessive thoughts. It's a process and you
are doing the hard work by learning mindfulness.
When you're committed to being here right now, you
will start to see the change in your behavior. It takes
time and you're doing it little by little. Big change
starts with small steps.

EXERCISE 4: ACCEPTANCE IS REFLECTED IN LANGUAGE

Acceptance is about recognizing and allowing what is here. The language we use can foster a sense of acceptance. Notice the feeling of "I want to go to the party, but I might get sick." Now notice the feeling of "I want to go to the party, *and* I might get sick." Do you notice a difference? For many people, "but" implies "I want to do something, but I'm not going to" whereas "and" implies "I'm going to do something, and this other thing might also happen." Try to change the language when your mind is creating thoughts about avoidance. Sometimes subtle shifts can make big differences. After trying it for a few days, reflect on anything you noticed.

EXERCISE 5: WEATHER SYSTEM

A visualization that provides a little distance from emotions and helps support the part of you that can observe thoughts and feelings without getting caught up in them is the weather system visualization. In this exercise, imagine yourself in a plane at 40,000 feet in the air. From that vantage point, you can see hurricanes, thunderclouds, the sun shining on the land, and cyclones moving across the face of the earth. You can watch them without getting caught up in them, so it is easier to accept that they are there, whereas if you were on the ground during a hurricane, it might seem that that was all there was. Bringing on an observing self that can witness your changing feelings, emotions, and thoughts is much like being at 40,000 feet and allowing what's there to change naturally.

MINDFUL MOMENT: ACCEPTANCE

While acceptance of anxiety is counterintuitive, it is also a crucial part of working with thought compulsions. If you're always in a boxing match with your thoughts, you can't very well play with your children, read a book, or do your job. If instead you take off your gloves and let your anxiety shadowbox with itself, you can be fully present in a life that takes on more and more vitality.

AFFIRMATION

I am surrendering to this moment and relin-

quishing control. I feel my feet on the ground

and my breath moving in and out of my body.

I am rooted in the truth of this moment and

I am open and ready for change. I can live with

OCD and it does not have to control who I am.

I am more than my disorder.

CHAPTER 5

Patience

THE CHALLENGE ························

Patience can help people living with OCD. When an intrusive thought pops into your mind, your instinct is to fight it, avoid it, or get rid of it. Any of these three reactions is understandable. But what if you do nothing? What if you just let the thought be there? That concept may seem foreign to you, but it is possible when using mindfulness. Being patient with yourself when you have a disturbing or intrusive thought may seem impossible, but you can learn to do it. One of the things you need to remember is that patience takes practice. Part of learning mindfulness is understanding the concept of self-compassion. If you automatically try to remove an intrusive thought from your consciousness when you have it, that's okay. Forgive yourself and understand that you are learning new techniques, and in that multilayered process it's crucial to have patience with yourself.

Common Obsessive Thoughts

Some intrusive thoughts center around the idea of having a disease or illness. Medical anxiety can be common among those who have OCD. Here are some examples of intrusive thoughts that center around having an illness or terminal disease.

> The bristles of my toothbrush aren't facing the same way as when I put it in the holder this morning. What if one of my roommates used it and they're sick? Now I'm going to get who knows what and there's nothing I can do about it.

> I have pain in my stomach. What if I have gastric cancer? I'm afraid that I've been ignoring signs that I have the disease, and now it's progressed to an untreatable stage.

> I forgot my therapy appointment. I must have dementia or Alzheimer's. It's progressing, and I'm afraid it's too late to get treatment.

> My hand is shaking and I'm sure it's not anxiety. It must be ALS or Parkinson's Disease.

> I'm afraid to take my medication because I'm sure it's going to cause me to develop a disease like cancer later in life.

Tammy's Story

Tammy is a mother of two young children. While taking them to school one morning, Tammy feels tightness in her chest. She's convinced that it's a heart attack. All she can think about is who will take care of her children if she dies. She's felt this tightness before and has gone to the emergency room, but each time they tell her that her heart is fine. Tammy thinks they missed something. She's afraid to tell her husband or her parents because they won't take her seriously this time. Tammy drops her children off at school and heads immediately to the ER. The doctors examine her, run tests, and yet again say that her heart is fine. They give her the business card of a therapist who specializes in anxiety. She feels embarrassed and ashamed and doesn't know what she's going to tell her husband about the ER co-payments they now owe.

How could Tammy use patience to help herself?

It's frightening to think that you might be having a heart attack. But Tammy doesn't have to jump to the conclusion that she's dying. She can be patient with her catastrophizing thoughts. Her chest tightness doesn't mean she's in cardiac arrest or at death's door. She can remember she's felt these sensations before and was told it was anxiety. Tammy can sit with them, feeling how they change, come, and go, and notice that when she doesn't fight against them, the feelings subside. She doesn't need to try to change her thoughts or feelings. She can be patient with what is going through her mind and understand that what she's experiencing is difficult, but that she has no obligation to act. Tammy can allow herself a few minutes alone to be with the sensations and then take a walk in a park, paying attention to what she sees, smells, and hears.

BREATH MEDITATION ·······································

You may have previously tried breath meditation, or you may have heard about it but avoided trying it. Take a moment to reflect on your experience or on the fears you might have about breath meditation and note them here.

_____

_____

_____

_____

_____

_____

_____

_____

_____

_____

_____

_____

_____

_____

_____

_____

_____

_____

_____

_____

We often have the tendency to think in terms of goals, and quickly reached goals at that. Meditation of any type requires patience and practice—patience with yourself when you realize how your thoughts jump around and how little control you have over them, and patience to continue practicing even when it's difficult.

Mindfulness meditation that uses the breath as the focus of attention is a foundation of meditation practice. The breath is always with us and is always available. It is an anchor you may return to at any time and in any place.

Begin by setting a timer for 10 minutes. Sit with your back straight but not rigid and your chin parallel with the ground, as though there's a string pulling you gently up from the top of your head. You may close your eyes, or if that's not comfortable, you may keep your eyes open and maintain a soft gaze at the floor a couple of feet in front of you.

Exhale as if you're blowing out birthday candles and then take a few deep breaths, exhaling each breath fully. Notice where the breath is most prominent for you: in the space between your upper lip and nose, on the outside of the nostrils, inside the nostrils, in the rising and falling of your chest, or in the rising and falling of your belly. Wherever you feel the breath most strongly, continue to use that same location as the focus of your awareness throughout this meditation.

The intention is to experience each breath as a unique event that will never happen again. Experience the in-breath, the pause before the out-breath, the out-breath, and the pause between breaths. The sensations are subtle, to be sure, but they are there and each one is unique.

When you hear the timer signal the end of the meditation session, slowly feel the sensations of your body against the chair, and when you are ready, you may open your eyes.

EXERCISE 1: WHAT HAVE YOU FACED BEFORE?

Whether through mindfulness or exposure, the treatment of OCD takes patience. Repeatedly opening up to and being curious about anxiety takes dedication, intention, and perseverance. What have you done in your life that required facing something difficult or persevering through discomfort in order to reach your goal? How were you able to be with the difficulties, and how might you use that experience to your benefit in this process of using mindfulness to help your OCD?

_____

_____

_____

_____

_____

_____

_____

_____

_____

_____

_____

_____

_____

_____

_____

_____

_____

Drawing from these strengths will boost your ability to engage in exposures.

EXERCISE 2: EXPOSURE PLANNING

Exposure is simply learning how to be with anxiety resulting from triggers in a different way, so there is no longer avoidance of those triggers. Much of your work on this path will consist of coming into contact with triggers in a planned or formal way, and learning how to work with spontaneous triggers that pop up during day-to-day living. Having a list of triggers from which to draw for formal exposure makes it easier to decide which to practice and gives you a sense of accomplishment when you see what you're able to do now that you weren't able to do in the past.

When you think about choosing a trigger for practice with formal exposure, consider it from the framework of whether you think you'll be able to be open to whatever experiences occur on a moment-to-moment basis during the exposure. Don't think about it from the standpoint of how much anxiety you believe it will cause, but consider whether you anticipate being able to be with the anxiety patiently. We can be in the presence of a trigger that causes a lot of anxiety, and that's fine, as long as we're willing to be with the anxiety in a mindful way. There's absolutely no shame in deciding that you're not willing to be with and work with certain sensations and emotions. This is where having a list of possible exposure triggers comes in handy. You may just pick another one that seems more approachable.

The benefit of mindfulness-based exposure is that you're learning a process. There's no need to get desensitized to each and every trigger you have. Once you're adept at the process, you can apply it anytime, in any situation. Patients have even reported that they've applied the same mindfulness techniques to other difficult emotions and are now living with greater ease in many ways.

Your OCD might exist in different subject matter areas (e.g., contamination, harm of self or others, religion, sex, or safety). Begin by listing, for each area, the thing you imagine would be the most difficult to approach mindfully (being open to the experience of sensations while disengaging from thoughts). Then come up with several in-between steps. For example, a mom with contamination fears who wants to take her children to the park to play might begin by writing the word "dirt" on a piece of paper. Sometimes just the letter "d" is enough to trigger anxiety. It doesn't matter what or how small the trigger is—this is completely personal. Perhaps her least approachable activity would be going to a spa and having a mud bath. Continue this process of listing for each of the OCD with which you struggle.

TRIGGER	CHALLENGING ACTIVITY

EXERCISE 3: MINDFULNESS-BASED EXPOSURE

You're learning a radically different way of approaching and experiencing your anxiety, which takes time. The guided meditations of sadness, anger, anxiety, and happiness, and how you feel them in your body, might have been an indication to you of how different this approach is from your usual way of being and how becoming increasingly expert at a mindful approach to anxiety is a process.

So, what's the nitty-gritty of exposure? Initially, once the trigger has evoked anxiety, you experience the physical sensations nonjudgmentally as they change from moment to moment. Notice your thoughts and let them be and dissipate on their own, without either arguing or agreeing with them. Bring your attention back to the physical sensations. In the beginning, while you're learning the process, you'll likely need to bring your attention back frequently. With practice and the willingness to feel whatever arises, you'll soon be able to engage with the experience and rest in whatever is present. Remember, you aren't necessarily aiming for a reduction in anxiety, although that is usually the happy byproduct. When you repeat an exposure, you're doing so in order to be more fully engaged with, and less defensive against, the experience.

For example, a mom with OCD concerning contamination might put dirt on her finger and be with the sensations while simultaneously noticing thoughts and returning her attention to the sensations. It's best to set a timer and commit to doing the exposure for the entire duration. It matters less how long the exposure lasts and more that it is a period of time during which you can keep the commitment to mindfully experience the anxiety. Of course, you won't relate to the anxiety in a mindful manner all the time, at least not at first. The commitment is to come back to mindfulness whenever you stray.

Now it's your turn. Pick a trigger from your list that seems relatively approachable. Follow the instructions for this exposure exercise and then write about your experience.

What was most difficult to be with?

What might you need to make room for in order to be more open to it in the future?

_____

_____

_____

_____

_____

_____

What surprised you about the experience?

_____

_____

_____

_____

_____

_____

What did you learn from the experience?

_____

_____

_____

_____

_____

_____

Encouraging Words

Patience isn't something you learn overnight. Remember that you're doing hard work when you step back and let your thoughts be there. It takes a lot of effort to be still rather than try to change your thoughts. Be patient with yourself during the process of learning mindfulness practice and you will begin to see positive results.

EXERCISE 4: WILLINGNESS

Let's look a little more closely at willingness. Willingness has often been compared to jumping. If I stand on a curb and touch one toe to the street, that's not jumping. Jumping by its nature requires both feet to leave the ground or surface. We can jump off a curb, off a chair, off a ladder. Each may involve different degrees of pain upon landing, but they are all jumping.

Willingness is like that. To set the intention of being willing to be with your experience means being fully open to it, accepting and inviting whatever arises in the moment. Even with that intention set, usually we'll close up or brace against an experience. The next time you are triggered by an intrusive thought and notice that you've become unwilling, be patient with yourself, set the intention of openness again and start over. With continued practice, your periods of openness will lengthen and the willingness to experience whatever is present will become what gives you the freedom to do the things that are important to you.

EXERCISE 5: AFTER THE EXPOSURE

In desensitization-type exposure, the method is generally to sit with the trigger until the anxiety goes down by at least half, then take a break, then repeat the exposure, and so on, until that trigger no longer causes anxiety. After that, the person would move on to the next trigger. Mindfulness-based exposure is different in that it is repeating an exposure for the sole purpose of becoming more and more willing to be with the experience—not to change it in any way or get space from the thoughts—and return to the present. Repeat the exposure with the trigger from the previous exercise with the intention to be even more open to the experience. There is no right or wrong number of times to do an exposure. Repeating is not failure. Repeating is further opening.

What did you notice when you repeated the exposure several times? How did your experience of the anxiety change?

MINDFUL MOMENT: PATIENCE

Many of us struggle with patience. We want instant gratification, and when we don't get it, we feel frustrated or defeated. One thing that can help you is knowing that patience isn't only about learning to wait. It's more about how you perceive the waiting process. When you're impatient, it's likely due to your attitude about having to wait. Remind yourself that waiting can be a reflective experience rather than a painful one. You can allow your mind to wander without trying to change its course. Patience is something we can learn by practicing mindfulness. The more you allow yourself to be in the present moment, without judging your experience or trying to change it, the more your tolerance for discomfort will improve. You will also notice a difference in your frustration levels and how much more patient you are with yourself than ever before.

AFFIRMATION

I am learning to trust myself during the process
of learning mindfulness exercises. By committing to the process of being in the moment,
I have already learned a valuable lesson
in patience.

Trust

THE CHALLENGE ···

One of the most challenging parts of OCD is that it can cause self-doubt. It's unsettling when you feel you can't trust yourself. You want to be secure in what you know, but everything seems uncertain. You question your thoughts, your ability to manage them, and sometimes what is real. Doubting yourself may make you feel alone or distressed much of the time. By practicing mindfulness, you develop a tool to use when you feel disconnected from the facts and what is real. Mindfulness grounds you in the present moment, and if you can't trust yourself at first, you can at least rely on the fact that you are here right now. That's a great start! From there, your trust in who you are and what you can do with mindfulness techniques can grow.

Common Obsessive Thoughts

Some obsessive thoughts people with OCD experience have to do with self-doubt. You may question what you know to be true, which is extremely distressing to someone with OCD. You don't know whether you did or did not do something. You wonder if you're a good or a bad person. Doubting yourself can make you feel out of control. Here are some examples of intrusive thoughts that center around self-doubt.

> I submitted my payment for my phone bill. I saw it on my bank statement, but I'm worried that my card was charged twice. I can't stop thinking that the phone company has my card information and they might charge it a second time.

> I had an argument with my daughter before she went to bed. I'm worried that she didn't hear me tell her I was sorry and that I love her. I know she's asleep now and I don't want to wake her, but what if she doesn't know that I apologized? What if she hates me and thinks I'm a terrible parent? I can never fix this problem.

> What if I'm a bad friend? What if my friends think I'm loyal but they're wrong? One day they're going to find out that I'm not a good person. I believe I try my best to be kind to my friends but I'm a fake. No matter what I do I can't change this.

Andy's Story

Andy is taking an exam for a college class in statistics. He's studied hard and he knows that he is prepared. He was struggling with the course at first and made an extra effort to get a tutor. The professor is intimidating, and Andy is worried that no matter how well he performs on the test, she'll think he is cheating. He is distracted during the test because he's sure that his professor thinks he's looking over his shoulder at another student's work. He can't shake the feeling that she's watching him and is going to accuse him of cheating on the exam. These intrusive thoughts are so distracting that he finds it difficult to answer the questions in front of him. He tries to push the thoughts out of his mind. When that doesn't work, he attempts to reassure himself that his eyes are on his test and nowhere else. He feels himself sweating because of how anxious he is and how he can't seem to stop the thoughts.

How can Andy learn to trust himself?

Andy knows that he studied hard for the exam. Trying to reassure himself by remembering all the effort he put into studying and that he's gotten good grades before doesn't work to get rid of his anxiety. What he can do instead is let the intrusive thoughts be there and trust that they are just thoughts. He doesn't have to prove anything to himself. The thoughts are trying to provoke him to doubt himself. He doesn't have to fall for it. Instead, he can focus on the work in front of him, let the thoughts wander through his mind, and remember that they are the result of his OCD. They are not evidence that he's cheating or that his professor doesn't trust him.

SELF-COMPASSION MEDITATION

Trusting in yourself when you have OCD can be a tricky matter. You aren't alone if you've ever wondered how you can possibly trust yourself when you can't even trust your thoughts. However, thoughts are just thoughts, a string of words hanging together, and not all of them deserve your time and attention. What *is* helpful to develop trust in is your ability to support and be kind to yourself. Because people often "battle" with their "OCD bully," it can be common to develop a hatred for that part of yourself; but if you're warring against a part of you, can you ever really win?

If instead you develop compassion for the pain you're in, you provide a wonderful support for yourself. The work of Kristin Neff, PhD, and Christopher Germer, PhD, in the area of Mindful Self-Compassion has been revolutionary. Please try this simple meditation, which is an adaptation of their work.

Sit with your back straight but not rigid and your chin parallel with the ground, as though there's a string pulling you gently up from the top of your head. You may close your eyes, or if that's not comfortable, you may keep your eyes open and maintain a soft gaze at the floor a couple of feet in front of you. Now take both hands and place them on your chest, either in the center or over your heart. Repeat the following phrases to yourself, letting them wash over you. Think of these as kind wishes for yourself: "May I live with ease. May I be at peace. May I be kind to myself. May I be healthy in body, heart, and mind. May I be free from suffering." Start by doing this meditation for 5 minutes a day and add time as you find it to be helpful. Remember that these are wishes for yourself; there is no requirement that you embody them already.

EXERCISE 1: DEFUSION

OCD involves the overvaluation of thoughts. They seem important, true, and urgent, but at the same time, although the thoughts are real, they might not *be* true. How can you get some space from thoughts that are not helpful? The work of Steven Hayes, PhD, Kelly Wilson, PhD, and Kirk Strosahl, PhD, in their development of Acceptance and Commitment Therapy (ACT), can provide a great deal of help. They use the term "fusion" to describe our tendency to become fused, like two pieces of metal soldered together, with our thoughts, believing that if we think it, it must be true and warrant our immediate attention. "Defusion" is the practice of recognizing thoughts as just thoughts and determining if a thought is helpful in a particular moment. For example, if someone is about to go into a party, repeatedly wondering or worrying about whether anyone there has a cold is probably not helpful in terms of enjoying the party.

One of the most useful tools for defusing unhelpful thoughts is to rewind and rephrase using the prompt "I notice I'm having the thought that . . ." Do you notice a different tone between "People at the party might be sick and I could catch it" and "I notice I'm having the thought that people at the party might be sick and I could catch it"? Often the first carries with it the sense that you'd better not go to the party, while the second says, "Yep, there's a thought, and not a particularly helpful one at that."

Use this defusion technique as frequently as you can when you find yourself stuck in thought, and allow yourself to trust in this process. It can also be helpful to use the technique with pleasant and neutral thoughts. Trying this exercise with all types of thoughts can benefit you.

Take a moment to write down your impressions of this technique after you've used it a few times.

EXERCISE 2: GRATITUDE

It can be difficult to trust that life will ever be any different. OCD can fill up so much time and mental space that the things you used to do and care about can seem lost in the fog. Even with the enormous suffering of OCD, there is still much in life that you can appreciate, and with that appreciation comes a realization that your life can be different.

A gratitude journal orients your mind to look for and appreciate things for which you are grateful. Make a practice of each day writing down five things for which you were grateful that day. They don't have to be big things; the feeling of clean sheets or hearing the birds in the morning or the smile of a child are all wonderful examples. As you write down each thing for which you were grateful, let the feelings of pleasure wash through you and trust that as you continue on this journey, you'll be more available to appreciate and bask in all the beautiful things that make up our world.

EXERCISE 3: MINDFUL CONVERSATIONS

Do you ever feel so distracted by OCD that you don't trust yourself to follow and participate in conversations? It's pretty tough to be present when your thoughts are spinning. Just about all of us have the tendency to formulate our response while the other person is still speaking, even if our thoughts aren't spinning. We leapfrog over what is actually happening in order to get to our future answer.

One mindfulness exercise that has numerous benefits is being truly engaged in conversation. That means noticing the other person's facial expressions, their posture, and other nonverbal cues. It also means really listening to what they're saying and taking it in without formulating your response. Only after they've finished speaking should you pause for a moment to think about your response. Participating in conversation in this way can be difficult in our society. Often people feel such an urge to get their piece out before the subject changes or before they are interrupted that they speak over one another. Acceptance that you might not get in everything you want to say can give you the freedom to experiment.

Beginning with one-on-one conversations, practice listening mindfully and then composing your response. See if it doesn't help you build trust that you can be with people in a more open and connected way.

Encouraging Words

Learning to trust yourself is a process. OCD can convince you that there are reasons to doubt what you know. It can be helpful to recognize that self-doubt is a common part of OCD. As you practice mindfulness more and more, you will have a greater sense of self and grounding. You will recognize that you are stronger than you thought you were. You will learn to trust what you know and how to handle situations as they come up.

EXERCISE 4: INFORMAL PRACTICES

Formal mindfulness meditation has myriad benefits. It's also true that informal mindfulness is beneficial. There are so many routine activities during the day that we can be with mindfully. This informal mindfulness practice builds trust that you can be with experiences in a different way, which is the crux of mindfulness-based OCD treatment. Choose a few activities with which to practice. Taking a shower is a great one. We often plan the day or think about problems when showering. Instead, try experiencing the feeling of the water on your body, the places that are cold and the places that are warm, the smell of the shampoo and soap, the feeling of the suds as you wash. Brushing your teeth is also a good one; the mouth is full of nerve endings. One of my favorites is mindful eating: Eat one bite of food at a time very slowly, experiencing the texture, temperature, and flavor in your mouth as you chew. How do these things change as you continue to chew? Not only does this particular activity provide multiple opportunities for mindfulness practice, but it has the bonus of truly savoring yummy food.

EXERCISE 5: ABCS AND DIVIDE BY THREE

Another informal practice to help focus the mind and move your attention toward present surroundings is a game you might have played as a child. Although very simple, the practice is surprisingly effective. Look around your current environment and find something that starts with the letter "A," then move through the rest of the alphabet. Change it up and begin from the middle of the alphabet or begin with "Z" and work your way backward. This informal practice brings you back to the present—you can only see what's in front of you at the present moment—and gives your mind something to chew on. When you have been engaging in thought compulsions, it can be helpful to have something present moment–oriented to bring your mind back to. This isn't meant to be a distraction, but rather an engagement with the present.

Another informal practice is to count backward from 100 by threes. Doing so engages the mind and allows for a present-moment challenge. As you practice mindfulness, it will become easier and easier to return your attention to whatever is present, no matter how subtle. In the beginning, however, it can help to have something with which to actively engage.

MINDFUL MOMENT: TRUST

Trust can be a struggle for people with OCD. The idea of trust relies on having faith, but you may feel as if you can't trust your thoughts or even yourself. When you first start to practice mindfulness, it may feel like it's not possible to trust in the process. You might wonder, "Is this going to work?" You never know what is going to happen in life, but you will learn that you can rely on these techniques. Trust that you have the tools to navigate intrusive thoughts. You are doing the best you can with the skills that you are working so hard to learn. Learning to trust in yourself and the process takes time, but understand that you are doing the hard work to benefit your life.

AFFIRMATION

Even though I have OCD, I love and accept
myself as I am. I'm learning to trust myself as
I embrace practicing mindfulness. There is
no time limit on how long it takes me to trust
myself. I am doing the best that I can with the
tools I have. I am open to embracing self-doubt
so I can learn to believe in myself and what
I know to be true.

CHAPTER 7

Non-striving

THE CHALLENGE ···

For people with OCD, it can be difficult to just be in the present moment. Many individuals ruminate on what happened in the past or what could occur in the future. It's common to get stuck on "What if" thoughts when you live with OCD because considering all the possibilities could be seen as a way to try to control the outcomes of situations. Unfortunately, we cannot think our way out of bad things happening. However, if you practice the mindfulness principle of non-striving, you can learn to quiet your busy mind and accept that you are here right now, in the present moment. It's okay to let your thoughts pass by without trying to change them. You might worry about the worst-case scenario, but you don't have to stop yourself from thinking. Let the thoughts be there. There's nothing wrong with you because you're having intrusive thoughts. People think all sorts of things, but it doesn't reflect on their character.

Common Obsessive Thoughts

In the previous chapters, we've discussed common intrusive thoughts that go along with OCD. Here are some further examples of intrusive thoughts.

> I touched a grocery cart at the store. What if someone with a virus used that cart? I must have the illness and I'm doomed. I'm going to die.

> My friend and I got into an argument and she said everything was fine, but I'm worried that she hates me. I can't stop thinking about the disagreement and wondering if I said something really offensive. She hates me and she's going to stop being my friend.

> My boss gave me an assignment and I'm worried that what I produced wasn't good enough. I'm having trouble sleeping because I can't stop thinking about the project. I must have messed it up somehow. What if I get fired?

Jane's Story

Jane watches a lot of documentaries on serial killers. Their minds are fascinating to her and she can't stop viewing these shows. After some time, she starts to think, "What if I like these stories because I'm a murderer?" She ruminates about the idea of her being a killer. She thinks, "I have to watch more shows to prove that I'm not like those people." She asks for reassurance from her friends: "Do you think I'm capable of committing murder?" She questions herself when she gets angry. She wonders if her temper is the sign of some deeper problem. No matter what she says or does, she is convinced that she is (or will become) a serial killer.

How can Jane use non-striving to help herself?

Jane is stuck in a pattern of ruminating and obsessing. Instead of trying to reassure herself that there's nothing wrong with her, she could practice simply being. Using mindfulness, Jane can focus on grounding techniques. She doesn't have to convince herself of her good moral character. The thoughts are upsetting, but they don't reflect on her in a negative way.

MEDITATION ON THOUGHTS ··············

Meditation on thoughts is, over time, extremely helpful with changing your relationship to obsessive thoughts and being able to move away from thought compulsions. Let's practice now.

Begin by setting a timer for 10 minutes. Sit with your back straight but not rigid and your chin parallel with the ground, as though there's a string pulling you gently up from the top of your head. You may close your eyes, or if that's not comfortable, you may keep your eyes open and maintain a soft gaze at the floor a couple of feet in front of you. Notice the points of contact between your body and the chair, feeling the warmth and pressure. In your own time, bring your attention to your thoughts. You don't have to alter your thoughts in any way; there are no right or wrong thoughts. As best you can, simply notice the thoughts as they pass through your mind, releasing the need to follow a thought with either agreeing or disagreeing thoughts. You might find it helpful to label the type of thought, gently saying to yourself "planning" or "worrying" or "remembering." Labeling can help you disengage from the content of the thought and see it as just a thought. If your mind quiets down, you may always turn your focus back to the breath until the next thought comes along. When the timer sounds, gently bring your attention back to the feeling of sitting in the chair, and when you're ready, you may open your eyes.

EXERCISE 1: REASSURANCE

As we learned in the example with Jane, thought compulsions can take the form of giving oneself reassurance (e.g., "I've never hurt anyone before. I must be okay."). Reassurance seeking can also take the form of a behavioral compulsion. It can be subtle and seemingly innocuous. What could be the harm in Jane asking her friends whether they think she is capable of murder? Just as with any compulsion, the harm is that it reinforces the notion that something must be done (in this case, asking for reassurance) in an attempt to make the anxiety go away and refuse to mindfully be with the feeling of anxiety. While seeking reassurance will likely reduce anxiety for a brief time, the next time the obsession comes to mind, the process will have to be repeated again. The first step is to notice that you're either giving yourself reassurance or seeking it from others. The second step is recognizing this reassurance seeking as a compulsion. During the course of the next week, notice the instances in which you seek to reassure yourself or seek reassurance from others, and write them down. There is some space here in which to write, but if you're like most people, you'll need to continue on a separate sheet. Because reassurance is both blatant (e.g., asking someone if they saw you do something, like turn off the stove) and subtle (e.g., talking to someone on the phone while walking by an elementary school because then there's no way you could molest a child unnoticed), it's important to practice recognizing when you seek it.

Reassuring Thought Compulsions

_____

_____

_____

_____

_____

_____

_____

_____

Seeking Reassurance from Others

_____

_____

_____

_____

_____

_____

_____

_____

_____

_____

_____

_____

_____

_____

EXERCISE 2: ENDING REASSURANCE SEEKING

Now that you've identified some of the ways in which you seek reassurance, either from yourself or others, it's time to learn what to do instead. If you engage in a reassurance thought compulsion, you may "undo" or "spoil" it by telling yourself, "It's possible, but there's no way to know for sure." If you found that you seek reassurance from others, you may ask them to say something along the lines of "I think you're asking for reassurance and that's not helpful. Can you sit with the anxiety or must you have reassurance?" whenever you seek reassurance. We don't want you to get into a power struggle with those in your support system, and we don't want them to become the Reassurance Police. But often just asking the question allows you to pause and determine whether you can in fact be with the anxiety. If you truly cannot in that moment, they can give you reassurance. It's not the end of the world, and at least you will be conscious of having sought reassurance.

Just reading this could have triggered some thoughts, such as:

> What if I can't stand it?

> What if the people from whom I seek reassurance actually begin recognizing it and asking me if I can sit with my anxiety?

> I don't think anyone recognizes what I'm doing. I don't want to clue them in!

Take a moment to note any thoughts that came up for you.

_____

_____

_____

_____

If any of these thoughts get in the way of you moving forward, work with them in the same way you've learned to work with other sticky thoughts (see page 8). The great thing about this exercise is that you're learning a mindfulness practice that can be applied to many things.

EXERCISE 3: RIDING THE SWELLS

A helpful way to frame the practice of learning how to manage your anxiety in new ways—instead of giving yourself reassurance or seeking reassurance from others—is thinking of it like riding the swells of the ocean, also known as urge surfing. If you stand stiffly against a swell, you'll be engulfed by water. If instead you are able to let go and let the water lift you up and then settle you back down, you can move through the swell with ease. Consider this the next time you experience anxiety. If you let go and let the anxiety move through you without fighting against it or trying to change it in any way, you will move through it with much greater ease.

Encouraging Words

In silence there is eloquence. Stop weaving and see how the pattern improves.

—Rumi

Sometimes it helps to embrace the silence. Sometimes people feel the pressure to keep talking to fill the space. Next time you feel that urge, stay quiet and let your thoughts be. You may be surprised at what you discover.

EXERCISE 4: FREEDOM

Remember the list of things you wrote that you want to do but haven't been able to do? Take a moment to review your list. Have you done any of them, even partially, so far?

_____

_____

_____

_____

_____

_____

_____

For those activities that are still on your list, make a plan to do exposures that will move you in that direction. (Remember that exposures are anything that brings you in contact with that which triggers anxiety.) How will you continue to move in your valued directions? Don't rush it; it's more important to practice openness and willingness than it is to speed through the process. Be kind to yourself and take the time to really get to know your experience. This is a good time to make some notes about how you will approach these things that you've been wanting to do.

_____

_____

_____

_____

_____

EXERCISE 5: FOCUS ON CHANGING THE RELATIONSHIP

It can seem like a bit of a paradox to suggest that non-striving can be beneficial and actually lead to a reduction in the amount of anxiety you feel. Of course, you want anxiety to be triggered less often and you want to be more functional in your life. But as you've seen throughout these pages, focusing on the reduction of anxiety in a particular exposure or situation generally leads to an increase in anxiety. If instead you focus on changing your relationship with the anxiety so that you may approach it mindfully, the happy byproduct is generally a long-term reduction in anxiety. So focus on the moment and relating to your anxiety differently and the rest will take care of itself.

Reflect on how you make sense of this for yourself and what your experience has been like practicing this radically different approach.

MINDFUL MOMENT: NON-STRIVING ················

Anxiety is all about the future. Just about any thought can be translated to "What will happen in the future?" or "How will I feel in the future?" OCD is interesting because this part of you cannot stand uncertainty, but only about particular things. You go through your day doing all kinds of things that don't come with a guarantee of certainty. If your OCD doesn't include obsessions about safety, you're able to walk out of the house without being certain that every plug has been unplugged. You're willing to accept that degree of uncertainty rather than spend an hour checking and rechecking. Our hope is that through the ongoing practice of the concepts in this workbook, you will feel increasingly comfortable with uncertainty about the future and will be able to fully engage in what's actually present in your life at this moment.

AFFIRMATION

I have the power to rise above my intrusive
thoughts. They may upset me, but they don't
mean that I am a bad person. I am practicing
simply being. I'm on a journey of self-discovery
and embracing my intrusive thoughts is a part
of that. I don't have to fix the thoughts, but
instead approach myself with compassion.

8

Letting Go

THE CHALLENGE ··

One of the challenges for those living with OCD is allowing the body and mind to release and relax. There is pressure to fix the "problems." With mindfulness, there is no pressure to stop the way you think. There's no right way to be, because who you are is fundamentally okay. Mindfulness helps us get to a state of acceptance. One key component of relaxation is to release and surrender yourself to the moment. You can do that by practicing mindful breathing exercises (see page 66). There are many other techniques you can use to allow your mind and body to relax, one of which is to focus on letting go. The mind-body connection is powerful, which you will discover when you focus on relaxation.

Common Obsessive Thoughts

Some common OCD thoughts involve the consequences for doing, or not doing, something.

> I had a thought about my coworker being lazy. They're going to know that I thought that about them. I have to tell them and apologize. If I don't apologize for my thinking, God will punish me.

> I'm worried about my child being molested by a pedophile. I've talked to her about inappropriate touching, but I'm afraid that no matter what I do or say, someone will hurt her. When I see the teachers at her school, I'm convinced one of them could be a pedophile.

> I paid my car insurance, but what if the card didn't go through? I got the receipt in my inbox and I can see it on my bank statement, but what if there was a mistake and the payment wasn't noted? I'm afraid that I'll get arrested for driving without insurance. The police are going to pull me over and they're going to take me to jail. Whenever I see a police car on the road, I'm sure they're after me.

James's Story

James has a college professor that he likes. He enjoys his philosophy class. Sometimes, he has difficulty focusing in class because he has flashes of inappropriate thoughts about the professor. James isn't attracted to him, but he has intrusive thoughts about being gay. He's never been attracted to men and is happy in his heterosexual relationship, but the obsessive thought triggers checking behavior and makes it extremely difficult to focus in class. He checks whether he is sexually aroused, whether he looks directly at the professor for too long, and whether he is looking at guys in the class more than he is looking at girls. Who can he tell about this? Not his girlfriend, because he's terrified she wouldn't understand and would break up with him.

How can James use letting go to help himself?

James is tempted to reassure his fears. Instead of trying to convince himself of his sexual orientation, he can let his thoughts flow and understand that they're a product of OCD. He can recognize that they make him feel bad but that he doesn't have control over them. He can trust that he's straight and let other thoughts dissipate on their own.

MEDITATION ON YOUR
EXPERIENCE AS A WHOLE ·······················

Begin by setting a timer for 10 minutes. Sit with your back straight but not rigid and your chin parallel with the ground, as though there's a string pulling you gently up from the top of your head. You may close your eyes, or if that's not comfortable, you may keep your eyes open and maintain a soft gaze at the floor a couple of feet in front of you. When you are ready, bring your attention to your breath for a few cycles. Then, rest your mindful awareness on your body as a whole. Be with the moment-to-moment experience of sitting. When your mind wanders, as it naturally will, gently guide it back to your present experience. When a sensation becomes prominent, turn your attention to it until it no longer dominates your field of awareness. For example, if you feel an itch, see if you can be with the sensations until they fade away on their own. It sounds strange, but they really will disappear without you doing anything about them. Perhaps you will notice your chest tightening. If so, turn your mindful attention to it to experience the sensations until they fade away, and then return to your experience as a whole. If you notice that you are caught up in thoughts, notice them mindfully and use the conveyor belt or popcorn popper techniques (see pages 26 and 24) if helpful. When the thoughts no longer pull your attention, return your awareness to your whole self, sitting.

How was this meditation different for you than the previous meditations? Was it more or less challenging? What types of sensation drew your attention? What types of thought drew your attention?

_____

_____

_____

_____

_____

_____

_____

EXERCISE 1: BENEFITS OF A REGULAR MINDFULNESS PRACTICE

You've been exposed to several different types of formal meditation practice over the course of this workbook. Continuing to practice the exercises will be a crucial part of working mindfully with your thought compulsions and OCD. In order to develop and maintain a regular practice, it's best to set a regular time of day for your practice. First thing in the morning is a popular time to meditate because it starts the day off with a mindful intention. In the evening before bed is also popular because meditation tends to quiet the mind and make it easier to fall asleep. Even the middle of the day is fine if that's what's most convenient for you. The time of day doesn't really matter. What's important is that you find a time when you can practice consistently. Start with 10 minutes a day and increase by increments of 5 or 10 minutes until you are regularly meditating for 20 to 30 minutes most days of the week. That may seem daunting now, but as you continue to practice, your meditation can become a refuge and place of stillness.

EXERCISE 2: DEVELOPING A REGULAR MEDITATION PRACTICE

In addition to having a consistent time of day for practice, it's also helpful to have a particular spot where you will be uninterrupted while meditating. It doesn't have to be a silent place, just somewhere you can settle into the practice. After all, if the space is particularly noisy, you can always do sound meditation!

What time of day would you like to set as your time for practice?

_____

_____

_____

_____

_____

Where is a good place to practice?

_____

_____

_____

_____

_____

Is there anything you can do to make that place feel more special?

_____

_____

_____

_____

_____

EXERCISE 3: SAVORING

Our minds are wired to focus on the dangerous or the seemingly dangerous. As psychologist Rick Hanson, PhD, says, "The brain is like Velcro for negative experiences, but Teflon for positive ones." The work you've undertaken is challenging and takes courage. There is real strength in being willing to be with that which scares you the most. Dr. Hanson's work in neuroscience is helpful in supporting our recognition and "velcroing" of the good. You can do this with a variety of things, but let's use the example of completing an exposure having felt open and mindful throughout the experience. Afterward, take just 30 seconds to close your eyes and let the feeling of accomplishment wash over you. This helps your mind associate positive feelings with completing an exposure. Doing this is a wonderful support for approaching anything difficult. Try this technique with all kinds of things. Perhaps you're able to meet with a friend and eat in a restaurant for the first time in years. Take a moment to let the feelings of connectedness, freedom, and accomplishment wash over you. Savor the feelings.

What did you notice when you practiced savoring the good? Are there times and situations in which you'd like to practice this?

Encouraging Words

When you're struggling with obsessive thoughts, remind yourself that there's a stillness in you that you can access at any time, wherever you are. Regardless of your physical location, you can practice mindful exercises. If you are walking down the street, pick a noise that you observe, focus on that sound while you walk, and tune out the rest of the world. Thoughts will come into and go out of your mind.

EXERCISE 4: FREEDOM

Remember the scale you completed at the beginning of the workbook? Without going back and looking at it, complete it again here. When you've finished, compare your scores. Mindfulness is something that develops over time, so please don't be discouraged if there isn't the change you'd hoped for. Come back every three months or so and see how your score changes over time.

THE MINDFUL ATTENTION AWARENESS SCALE (MAAS)

The Mindful Attention Awareness Scale (MAAS) will give you an indication of your current degree of mindfulness. To complete this scale, please give your answers in terms of how you have felt over the past week.

Rate the following statements on a scale from 1 to 6.
1: almost always 2: very frequently 3: somewhat frequently
4: somewhat infrequently 5: very infrequently 6: almost never

_____ 1. I might feel an uncomfortable emotion and not be conscious of it until later.

_____ 2. I'm distracted and forget where I put things like my keys or my bag.

_____ 3. I'm often lost in the past or the future.

_____ 4. When walking, I'm usually unaware of my surroundings.

_____ 5. I have a vague sense of discomfort in my body, but it's difficult to identify the sensations.

_____ 6. I often find it difficult to pay attention in conversations.

_____ 7. I'm on autopilot most of the time.

_____ 8. When I am doing something, I'm thinking of the next thing I have to accomplish.

_____ 9. It's difficult to focus on what I'm doing in the moment because I want to get to the end.

_____ 10. I do compulsive behaviors automatically.

_____ 11. I only listen with one ear because I'm preoccupied with my thoughts.

_____ 12. I walk into a room and then forget why I'm there.

_____ 13. I will look down and see an empty plate, hardly having been aware of eating or of the taste of the food.

_____ 14. I feel the need to push away disturbing thoughts so that I can pay attention.

_____ 15. I get lost in thought compulsions and time goes by without my realizing it.

Total score of the 15 items: _____

Your beginning score: _____

EXERCISE 5: HOW HAS YOUR PERSPECTIVE CHANGED?

Congratulations on working your way through this book! This isn't easy work, but the rewards are tremendous. You've viewed anxiety and OCD from a very different perspective and have been brave enough to try new things. How has your perspective about struggle, mindfulness, and anxiety changed over the course of this work? Which insights and exercises have been the most helpful for you and how can you support yourself in continuing the practices?

MINDFUL MOMENT: LETTING GO

When a person with OCD has intrusive thoughts, they feel the need to try to control them. There are many ways an individual might do this. They might try to reassure themselves that the bad thing they worry will happen isn't probable. The person might fixate on the problem and try to solve it. Another component of obsessive thoughts is the element of shame; as if it wasn't bad enough to think disturbing things, the person now feels worse that they thought about those upsetting concepts in the first place. They might beat themselves up over their privilege to worry about such things or wonder why they can't stop. These sorts of thoughts and behaviors can lead to frustration, heightened stress levels that make OCD symptoms worse, or even panic attacks. So what can you do in a situation in which you want to control your thoughts but can't?

The solution is to remember that you don't have control. The answer is to let go. Hearing the words "let go" might make you feel incredulous—how can you let go of a disorder that feels uncontrollable? We know it sounds counterintuitive, but letting go will help you manage your OCD. Your thoughts are going to be there. Acceptance and compassion work together. The first step is to accept that you're having these thoughts; once you accept that you're experiencing the thoughts, you can move toward self-compassion. Remember, living with OCD can be painful, and it's crucial to acknowledge the validity of how it feels to have intrusive thoughts. When you notice yourself becoming angry or frustrated, that's the time to be gentle with yourself. You did not choose to have OCD, nor did you select the thoughts in your head.

AFFIRMATION

I give myself credit for the difficulty of the
moment I'm experiencing. I understand that all
I can do is all I can do, and that is good enough.

9

Onward, Upward

FINDING WHAT WORKS FOR YOU ·················

As you know, everyone's OCD manifests differently. Similarly, the treatment and mainte-
nance of OCD is going to be unique for every individual. As you try out different tactics
for coping with your OCD, do not be ashamed if certain things don't work for you. Most
important, don't let a lack of results from one technique stop you from trying something
else. With this workbook and any other resource, take what works for you and leave what
doesn't. Doing so will allow you to find a sustainable way to cope with OCD long term and
deal with the ebb and flow of the condition.

Remember, with OCD, there will be days when you struggle with your thoughts. Nothing
in life is perfect, and managing Obsessive-Compulsive Disorder is challenging. In addition to practicing mindfulness, it's important to see a licensed therapist if you are having
trouble dealing with your OCD. Someone who specializes in the condition can help you
understand what you're struggling with and help you develop effective coping techniques. Mindfulness may be a part of this process. You can take the techniques that you've
found in this workbook to therapy and work on them with the help of a licensed mental
health professional. That way, you will have support as you work on issues that you have
surrounding obsessive thoughts. Remember that taking it day by day, or even moment by
moment, can help with OCD. You are more than your thoughts.

SHORT-TERM OUTLOOK ·······················

Getting to a better place with your mental health isn't a linear progression. Regardless of
whether a person has OCD or not, they're going to have harder times and easier times in
life. For a person with a mental disorder, those hard times can trigger old behaviors and
thought processes, and normal life stressors or difficult events come with an additional
hardship. This workbook is here to help you build a toolbox of skills, and just as healing isn't linear, this book doesn't have to be used in a way that is linear. You can return
to any of the exercises as many times as you want or need; in fact, revisiting them often
may help you make them concrete coping skills that are more likely to come to the fore-
front immediately when challenges arise. The more you practice using coping skills and
mindfulness, the more they'll become your default modes and serve as a foundation for
managing your OCD.

Mindfulness is about being in the moment, a crucial skill for those with OCD. When you are ruminating or in the midst of an obsession, it can be hard to remember that it will end. You can practice urge surfing (see page 5) or accepting the reality that intrusive thoughts are upsetting and disturbing. This workbook was created to help you build skills. Healing doesn't happen overnight, but the more you engage in mindfulness practices, the easier they'll become and the better you'll get at using them.

LONG-TERM OUTLOOK

OCD is biologically based, which means that it isn't a condition that "goes away." It is, however, one that you can learn to manage. Mindfulness is a strategy you can access at any time. By practicing the exercises in this book, you can reduce the anxiety and distress associated with intrusive thoughts. There is no cure for OCD, but the strategies you have learned within these pages can support you in managing the symptoms.

Although mindfulness focuses on the present, you may wonder what will happen after you've practiced this technique for an extended period of time. It's likely that your focus will be better at work and that you'll be less distracted when you're with your loved ones. There are so many different uses for mindfulness, all of which will help you manage your OCD.

Mindfulness is a lifelong practice. The more you work at it, the better you will feel. You can return to this workbook at any time. Practice any of the exercises that resonate with you. We hope that you have gained at least a few solid techniques to use when experiencing OCD symptoms or even just everyday life stressors.

RESOURCES

· · · · ·

WEBSITES

Anxiety and Depression Association of America. ADAA.org.

Association for Contextual Behavioral Science. ContextualScience.org.

Center for Mindful Self-Compassion. CenterForMSC.org.

"Center for Mindfulness." UMass Memorial Medical Center. UMassMemorialHealth care.org/umass-memorial-medical-center/services-treatments/center-for-mindfulness.

Chris Germer. ChrisGermer.com.

Hayes, Steven. "Acceptance & Commitment Therapy (ACT)." Association for Contextual Behavioral Science. ContextualScience.org/act.

International OCD Foundation. IOCDF.org.

Sage Psychotherapy. SagePsychotherapy.org.

Self-Compassion. Self-Compassion.org.

BOOKS

Brach, Tara. *Radical Acceptance: Embracing Your Life with the Heart of a Buddha.* New York: Bantam, 2003.

Germer, Christopher K. *The Mindful Path to Self-Compassion.* New York: Guilford Press, 2009.

Harris, Russ. *The Happiness Trap: How to Stop Struggling and Start Living.* Boston: Trumpeter Books, 2008.

Hayes, Steven C., and Spencer Smith. *Get Out of Your Mind and Into Your Life: The New Acceptance and Commitment Therapy.* Oakland, CA: New Harbinger, 2005.

Kabat-Zinn, Jon. *Full Catastrophe Living.* New York: Dell, 1990.

Kornfield, Jack. *A Path with Heart.* New York: Bantam, 1993.

McKay, Matthew, John P. Forsyth, and Georg H. Eifert. *Your Life on Purpose: How to Find What Matters and Create the Life You Want.* Oakland, CA: New Harbinger, 2010.

Neff, Kristin. *Self-Compassion: The Proven Power of Being Kind to Yourself.* New York: William Morrow, 2011.

Orsillo, Susan M., and Lizabeth Roemer. *The Mindful Way through Anxiety: Break Free from Chronic Worry and Reclaim Your Life.* New York: Guilford Press, 2011.

Schwartz, Jeffrey M., and Beverly Beyette. *Brain Lock: Free Yourself from Obsessive-Compulsive Behavior.* New York: ReganBooks, 1996.

Wilson, Kelly G., and Troy DuFrene. *Things Might Go Terribly, Horribly Wrong: A Guide to Life Liberated from Anxiety.* Oakland, CA: New Harbinger, 2010.

REFERENCES

· · · · · ·

American Psychiatric Association. *Desk Reference to the Diagnostic Criteria from DSM-5.* Arlington, VA: American Psychiatric Association, 2013.

Borchard, Therese J. "Non-Judging, Non-Striving and the Pillars of Mindfulness Practice." PsychCentral. Last modified July 8, 2018. PsychCentral.com/blog/non-judging-non -striving-and-the-pillars-of-mindfulness-practice.

Brown, Kirk W., and Richard M. Ryan. "The Benefits of Being Present: Mindfulness and Its Role in Psychological Well-Being." *Journal of Personality and Social Psychology* 84 (2003): 822–848. doi.org/10.1037/0022-3514.84.4.822.

Cirino, Erica. "10 Tips to Help You Stop Ruminating." Healthline. Accessed March 23, 2020. Healthline.com/health/how-to-stop-ruminating.

A Conscious Rethink. "6 Affirmations to Repeat When You're Overthinking." Last modified October 25, 2019. AConsciousRethink.com/3702/6-affirmations-repeat-youre -overthinking.

Gasnier, M., A. Pelissolo, G. Bondolfi, S. Pelissolo, M. Tomba, L. Mallet, and K. N'diaye. "Mindfulness-Based Interventions in Obsessive-Compulsive Disorder: Mechanisms of Action and Presentation of a Pilot Study." *L'Encéphale* 43, no. 6 (December 2017): 594–599. doi.org/10.1016/j.encep.2016.10.004.

Harris, Russ. *The Happiness Trap: Stop Struggling, Start Living.* Auckland: Exisle Publishing, 2007.

Hayes, Steven. "Acceptance." Association for Contextual Behavioral Science. Accessed February 5, 2020. ContextualScience.org/acceptance.

Hayes, Steven. "Cognitive Defusion (Deliteralization)." Association for Contextual Behavioral Science. Accessed February 5, 2020. ContextualScience.org/cognitive _defusion_deliteralization.

Hayes, Steven C., Kirk D. Strosahl, and Kelly G. Wilson. *Acceptance and Commitment Therapy: The Process and Practice of Mindful Change*, 2nd ed. New York: Guilford Press, 2012.

Hershfield, Jon, and Tom Corboy. "Mindfulness and Cognitive Behavioral Therapy for OCD." Accessed March 23, 2020. IOCDF.org/expert-opinions/mindfulness-and-cognitive-behavioral-therapy-for-ocd.

Kissen, Debra. "How to Take the Power Back from Intrusive Thought OCD." ADAA. Accessed March 23, 2020. ADAA.org/learn-from-us/from-the-experts/blog-posts/consumer/how-take-power-back-intrusive-thought-ocd.

Masuda, Akihiko, Michael P. Twohig, Analia R. Stormo, Amanda B. Feinstein, Ying-Yi Chou, and Johanna W. Wendell. "The Effects of Cognitive Defusion and Thought Distraction on Emotional Discomfort and Believability of Negative Self-Referential Thoughts." *Journal of Behavior Therapy and Experimental Psychiatry* 41, no. 1 (2010): 11–17. doi.org/10.1016/j.jbtep.2009.08.006.

Mindfulness Based Happiness (blog). "The 9 Attitudes of Mindfulness according to Jon Kabat-Zinn." MindfulnessBasedHappiness.com/the-9-attitudes-of-mindfulness-according-to-jon-kabat-zinn.

Santorelli, Saki F., ed. "Mindfulness-Based Stress Reduction (MBSR): Standards of Practice." The Center for Mindfulness in Medicine, Health Care, and Society. February 2014. Accessed March 23, 2020. UMassMed.edu/contentassets/24cd221488584125835e2eddce7dbb89/mbsr_standards_of_practice_2014.pdf.

Serani, Deborah. "An Introduction to Acceptance and Commitment Therapy." *Psychology Today*. February 22, 2011. PsychologyToday.com/us/blog/two-takes-depression/201102/introduction-acceptance-and-commitment-therapy.

Singer, Janet. "OCD and Mindfulness." PsychCentral. Last modified October 8, 2018. PsychCentral.com/lib/ocd-and-mindfulness.

ACKNOWLEDGMENTS

I'd like to thank my mom, Dorothy Kirk, who is and will always be my hero. A great deal of appreciation goes to my coauthor, Sarah Fader, for being a wonderful and fun collaborator. I also want to acknowledge the team at Callisto Media for their help and guidance. My friends provided wonderful support throughout the process and enriched my life on a daily basis.

Robin Taylor Kirk

I want to acknowledge my incredible coauthor and clinician, Robin Kirk. Robin, you were a joy to work with and I loved learning from you. Thank you to the team at Callisto Media, including our editors Crystal Nero and Ashley Popp, for believing in us. I am endlessly grateful to my parents, who cheered me on through this journey, and my children, Ari and Samara.

Sarah Fader

ABOUT THE AUTHORS

Robin Taylor Kirk, LMFT, has been in the mental health field for 25 years and specializes in the treatment of anxiety disorders, including Obsessive-Compulsive Disorder, Social Anxiety, Body-Focused Repetitive Behaviors, Avoidant/Restrictive Food Intake Disorder, Panic Disorder, specific phobias, and generalized anxiety. In her private practice, Robin works with individuals and groups in addition to providing workshops and consultation for professionals. Robin developed Sage Anxiety Treatment Program, the first intensive outpatient program in the United States to offer strictly ACT-based ERP.

She also volunteers with the Buddhist Pathways Prison Project teaching mindfulness meditation to inmates.

Sarah Fader is the founder and CEO of Stigma Fighters, a nonprofit organization that encourages individuals with mental illness to share their personal stories. Her work has been featured in *The New York Times*, *The Washington Post*, *The Atlantic*, Quartz, BetterHelp, ADAA, Psychology Today, The Huffington Post, HuffPost Live, The Good Men Project, The Mighty, Ravishly, YourTango, and *Good Day New York*.

CPSIA information can be obtained
at www.ICGtesting.com
Printed in the USA
JSHW021701140720
6683JS00008B/245

9 781647 392383